T0150835

Alisoun Sings

Final volume in a trilogy of works using medieval and contemporary sources and languages. All published by Nightboat.

Meddle English (2011)
Drift (2014)

Alisoun Sings

NIGHTBOAT BOOKS / NEW YORK

Caroline Bergvall

Copyright © 2019 Caroline Bergvall
Printed in the United States
ISBN 978-1-64362-001-5
Cover art: Collage of detail from
The Ellesmere Chaucer, ca. 1400–1410,
mssEL 26 C 9, The Huntington
Library, San Marino, California
Designed by Crisis
and typeset in Mrs. Eaves
Cataloging-in-publication data is
available from the Library of Congress
Nightboat Books
New York
www.nightboat.org

Preface

It starts with a name. We pronounce her name. It rings across the room and disappears down the corridors of time. It disperses across spaces, travels through folded mineral lives, and comes to rest softly, a heartbeat waiting to be picked up. It matters little at this stage where the name comes from and whether it belongs to a historical, a mythical or a literary figure. What matters is the network of resonance that it brings up. What matters is its capacity to pull up events, sceneries, struggles as well as crowds of contradictory, marvellous, spirited beings in its sonorous wake. We call her name. She hears us calling. It rings out from many cycles, past and future set in motion. A voice starts to speak.

For years from then on it will be my stubborn task to listen for this voice, and transcribe or compose what she says, and keeps on saying, and try to get what it is it wants from me. All my attention and skills now tuned to the depths like a vast sensory receptor whenever the veils of time draw thin.

As a female lead, Alisoun resonates as one of the more provocative and talked about voices in the vast riches of Chaucer's medieval pilgrim tales. Yet every naming is both an affirmation and a holding station. Tales lead to more tales. Stories get woven from multitudes of stories. Voices call up other voices. A voice is a voice-cluster. I sense her coming through as a concert of sounds and lives and purposes from a vast patchwork of influences, events, and emotions that accord with her, and revitalise her presence among us. Her persona, her phrasing, her intentions, her clothes, her geographies, emerge, available, recyclable and drawn out from the infinite details and impulses of a great range of cultural, personal, physical even psychological reaches and attractions.

Perhaps some names are best suited for some epochs to carry out their mission. Our own times are caught in a vertigo of excess, dilapidation, barbarism, bad reality, and despair. Times of fear, fog and unsympathetic doctrines. We call out many names, high and low, for assistance, for guidance. We need purpose and service. We need exploits, boldness, inventiveness, strong joys. Most of them no longer bother answering the call. Aye, but listen up. A voice signals from within the noise. Then she starts to sing.

Alisoun
Sings

Dame

Hi you all, I'm Alisoun. Some people call me Al. Am many things to many a few thyinge to some & nothing but an irritant to socialites and othere glossing troglodytes. I dig a good chat banter aboute. Sbeen a long time, some & six hundred times have circled round the solar sun, everything were diffrent yet pretty much the same, sunsets were reddier, godabov ruled all & the franks the rest. Womenfolk were owned trafeckt regulated petted tightlye impossible to run ones own afferes let alone ones mynd nat publicly nat privatly, & so were most workfolk enserfed, owned never free, working working day 'n niht. Sunsets redder, legs a little shorter.

I've done well, sey so meselfe. Have traded textiles and vows fashioned millinery birdnestings as fine as Philip Treacy, halo creations brighte proude than Frangelico. Standing tall kept me upright saved me from oblivion, will get back to hats. Many a fine frockery have I cut & worn some even with buttons running all the way doun & upround again. Nodout for sure ma style wer too loud for sum, have been called any fin from scarecrow to fake cnight, what fakery? what knihtery? I play it large and bold, travel the distance forshure, nat grene as Gawain, the citys ma domayn, I'm Dame Alisoun Alys Ali Alyson. As for dress I take all ma Qs from Getalife, will get back to what.

Likeso have steered ma life a stourdy mount, life-part-nered once, lit that match, and a few more. Eeasier sayd thane doon but ne will have lovemakes plow ma jarden wivout chek-ing out t instrumnts & the mental state of their flowering. In ma team I made ma bed reel bizzy a stretch a streowen for many leien in, yoohoo we did! bountyful booties ov all kinds & kins entwined revling ydizzied, in nightly prospectings we made liht of the derke.

Say-so maself sbeen good, spite a beating, or two.

Vita

Ther comes a time in everyones lief whan 'tis gode think on ones condition & look ahead by looking in. Make sure this last stretch ylived in the most fulleste bestest manner prior to the grand Datsit. Call in the cards ones delt, shake ones tree for unwelcome guests gustes ghosts, and if possible empart the few purls one has managed to pluck from ones great sea of expedience. Nodout turning thrittitwenti is good timing. A time to speech ma minding 'n let some wisdam yrise. Call on a friendly assembly for fair share & witnessing, and there let ones hair down! Open ones mutt & shower the worlde until hoarse with wonder & insult! The artist Marina screamed until no voice & screamed some mo until the earth joined in. Ah the wonder! ah the insults!

Copyist

Do allocate someone to copy exchanges in your partee or you'll find that ne can make heads nor tales of whatswhat after awhile can lead all kinds of misreadings & typos oons th' ink has dried. And what with inattention, coffee stains, drippings and the likes, unfortunates pellings get tuff to hiden or changen, like bad tatts covering bad tatts, as chaucer the aufeur famously bemoaned.

Lingo

Btw nat worry should ma language feeling it weirdo, rude & cueryous at first. Rough as a cats lick or like a dress whats travagant, folded over updoubled, as though am speechin many langages at once. Whats foshur! And many stories too! In many gay apparel! Picture me standing on each side of the silver cliffs of Cinque & Caletum like standing at Midlina across the silfra crack, am astride the world joining two moats, the northern sea rushing between my herculean legs splashes against the mixed wools of my quim. No but for serious, 'tis a rich scrambljumbl of heavily crossbedded bitching tongues, folded like shells in tymologick tension, so is ma usage a happy combimess, simpel.

Ocourse right from the begun, language both connecks and divides, like a beefy stewed or a bukkenade sgot us carved up into dishes n gloseries, named ma kind for a specifick seafood, a pungent spice, leaves much out of the sauce, according to crockery hierachies, keep this one in this one out for freshness, usefulness, dominant criteria, & makes a master meal for a High Table none of us binvited to!

Teller

Sure languages cool for tally and keeping a counts of deeds and misdeeds, and thats allrighdy. Its changeable energy whats right enough for me. And no future achademye can ever change fact that ma tongue is as agile with it as a french kiss or a sailing cog in the storm. Anyways when comes to speeching and telling, no need for perfeck, nor for clevrest. Whoever needed sore long words anyways, like that giant protein made up of 189,819 letters what takes 4 hours to pronounce? Ive gotta traders grammar, lovers declension, indeedy me loins may stoppe blede, will get to that, but ma lovejuice is out of this worlde, has just begun aflowe the banks and whan I speech like this ma thoughts & aventures, tis like I am ysitting the lap of Sherazade & she axe for it 2 be longe 2 be loude, thats my whole megafony! Minde yow these dayes ofen wishe ma weight of talent can prophesise like a Cassandra, provoke uprisings liche Bouddicca and runne molten lava all over this Trompeii!! I hope whats clarified it? No foolery. Ma word's ma bond. Ma name's Alison, Dames Alison.

Assembly

Lo! hangon! give me liht, hold atorch! sayeth Ali lookie round. Everywhere I go hear about a range of movements n battles for social revolution for love & respeck & swich human diuersitie, all manner of this that & the other dimensions, time sup! enough senough! are a-rioting a-gathering on all kinds of squares and frequencies. Wat serious glosage n causes in groups & cells of selves, deep corage for deep psycho rev groping together, pushing the homefront out in all fields and croppings am majorly impressed yea should be dancing! Course for certayn nis all what gold glitters.

Emma

Tis like ha said ma mie Emma Goldman a greate lasse free-dom fighter, if I cant dance I dont wanna be part of yr rev! "Tis on the homefront it beginne womenfolks development hir freedom hir independance come from and through one-

self", sayd she, who poked & preacht & reproacht, fighted &
paid a high price for a whole lot of decent raving.

Gina

I know this well have got a big front too, fesses Ali, cant deny
Ive got appetite for fightinge for homing good faitability & a
better libbeing liveing libbed loved libated librated living for
mi selven & for alle. "I've always detested bullies, I've never
been afraid to stand by my words and deeds", seys ma friend
Gina not milling any wordes nor fierce braverie of mind,
"I've been quite used to being the most hated woman in the
investment and charity sectors but now I've been called the
most hated woman in the country".

Pussy

Aye, forsure, seyen his pussy comrades, femaled types called
out on the question of fredam. We more freere thanne ours
modres for sure & freere than ours granmothres for certeyn,
who bled the way and muchel sacrifice so we could choose a
lyfe. How much noize to be heard! How much attitude will
make any diff to the cultural imprint! How builden memory
from our continuity! Whats for shure not for show applies

by laws & degrees, depends on territories, changing political & religious estates, priests and cartels, even family histories. Tis all bout borderd controls, lectric fencing, walls being raised overniht, agendas are set all the way underskin. Femlaik embodied are boned deboned bashed to poulpe, pounded pissed on dragged drugged removed. Violent fliquée full of flippin' eruptions n rerun. Much open to abusage, dont protect cont protest, whipped lashed and beheaded for self defending.

Ykes, woman still a no-go zone! xlaims Alisoun, respeck & fredam muchel needing redress.

Jewel

How free of body heart & thought one is, how free of humours curses spells gosts putdowns and fears one be, how free to action labour love & politicks one be, how free to roam to lead to think to know otherwisely, to say-so publicly, how free to lead, to pushback, to love & lover, to marry to other, to mother to alter one is, how free to gedup and say No free to say-so, seye otherly! seye lookie round seye whats not right whats not riht, how free to alter the world, to change the wurdes falter the workes. How free extenden all being in hire being, femele male en melee. And finde hirselfe acompassed, at the stillpoint of the universe, s/he is point zero, full empty, neutral automatic, illuminate deep currents, unlocke chaines of power, offre radikly differentes emurgent solutions. How free to be a full person, how fully free to be a fre personne can one be, dear Bejewled.

Earthly Delights

Experience shows, continues Alisoun, everyone is spawned in 3D yet pruned in 2D, every singled ones of us are wooed groomed for specific agenders in this flatland & never be anyoon free of its games & curses. Folk be arranged one typer pair, an army for nought, a science of zeroes & ones, detach apply the repetitive blocks of exes, whys and zebras & 'member ne give a fig takes for king that which bulges roundly and for queens that which holds in place squarely, strictest two-pronged situation, its a structure for industry innit, a logic of global trading & worship, from bedrooms to boardrooms, aye what a wastage of good opps & positions!

Alphabete

Indeedy don know any oon born O but once becomes O stays strictly so, can never be fully self after that nor develop in peace by piece, in fact can only ever stand in for bits of oneself, nor on any accounting will there ever be fertile love nor lineage tween O & O, nor can an O be an A nor an XXY nor an XXL. All wat rules our design be locked into a two-lettered alphabete, and everybodys walking around gloved armoured silenced in it, "in a world so crassly indifferent to the various gradations and variations of gender and their great significance in life" quod Emma. One can be lucky with duties of self & shared care but love as a dremteam of equals frankly rarely expected here.

The tale of John Eleanors trial

Ther is the tale, muchel quoded of John Eleanor Rykeners trial broughte to the London courts in thirteenfourandninety on accusations of sexual misconduct. The problem was not the sex work. Nor the wanton membre. The problem was that the court did not know whether or not sodomy was committed. The court did not know, or could not decide, because they could not decide whether or not Eleanor is man or womman. She gives hir name as Eleanor, a propre queenly name, but after interrogacion, is forced to confess that she lived once as a man named John. In the end, a verdict not be recorded and the text accounte both the names "Eleanor" and "John" in Latin, switch allowed a neutral pronoun. Many such stories abounden of sexual richesse & its problems wit the lawe. Many with more dire consequences.

Spring of atoms

Yit in the joya of lyfe we all be related if diffirently, exlaims Alisoun. And showers soote suffuse all of our veins, mineral vegetal animal elves fairies cyborgs aliking hypacharged particles disperse unannounced cluster visions like dandelion snow & mathematical dances & all of the world's minds is irrigating all of our brains with life. A cellular haunting takes root humoids follow all way to the interior where holodecks spawn futured matter from a fountain of space to grow from the starship and love this starship by over seven million species, to be exact three-hundred-ninety-thousand-nine-hundred types of plants known to science & whats not counting the fisshes nor the mammals nor the insects nor the reptiles! So what if every thing is really nothing but a secret balancing of sentient matter, tangible intangible both, in front of such arousing atomiks all transforms can brek free & poetic bios like me can again find their plentifull place, like you woudnt know it but there are around ninety types of begonias around. So now, how many legs and limbs really do make a sphere, quod Alysoon, our knowledgeable guide through these leaves.

Atalanta

Indeedy glorious is this forest of forms yet now so ravaged & alien, how are one to know in troth which one to inhabit & pursue, which one be a real possibility, which oon a dated morpho-karmic entity. Survival depends on passing through all sorts of vital forms, camouflaging to heal, masking to reveal, passing to shine through, camouflaging to seduce. How would one know ultimately what in me knows intimitly, which one to manifest in fully open-thoated song? Every form be atomic every shape plastic. Despite scars of wounds what redirect emotion arounding cnots of hardness trauma, really thare hundreds & hundreds & thousands of possibilities. Each tree each bird each human each cloud each lion an emprisoned atalanta, each nightingale a released philomela, each cockroach an ancient lispector, each firefly a luminous pasolini! What one could be, might have been, might still be released into, like a frosc exploding at the sight of the vasteste oshun, or the worlde reveled in a seventeen sillable plop.

One sacred cow

Or what if I present as a cow, real cow, real ku, ancient &
wyse, born out of a sacred belch, rises from oceans of trash
and insults, ancient as freya, or nandini, ma boob collection
is heavy and strong can carry entire populations at their
handles, but pushed too far I become an angry bull & mount
entire cities to oblivion.

Two sacred cows

What if I present as a pair of divine cows, sacred lovers in
artichoke fields, diverse in form free to chew, femaled to-
gether, ancient & wise and not be stoned or jailed o kickd for
it, not to die for just one kiss nor getting 50 lashes for wearing
tha trousa nor being thrown out of planes or being dunked
in jail for using oons mouth as freshly as colpaste, as freely
as water runs & birds sing, for mouths I have a-plenty all over
me surface, for kissing ma beloving and singen swetlie mel-
odies on the wire, bird to bird bard to bard!

Three sacred stars: sh1n1ngbr1ghtly

And what if I present the three graces as new muses, 'tis a
count of 1-2-3, heady sky daughters stubborn teachers a stel-

lar roadmap, like ancient grammar thats one beyond the twos
might break the mould, starts the spiral pattern, of long and
short variations, arbitrary composites, like sunflower seeds,
no ending to the galaxies open up the polyamory of action,
lust for lyfe, Maesia Afrania Hortensia, sister constellations,
Body Mind Spirit, Alicia Garza, Patrisse Cullors, Opal To-
meti, star for star, shInIngbrIghtly, whatever else they'll tell
yous about female corage and gossibes, no need to go it alone,
use constellated guides the sterres in the frosty nyght, a stellar
map of care & disobedience, and sail on your chosen ship of
friends!

A field: constellation

Wat if I present as a crowd, a school of beings deep and el-
emental, wisdom aroused, skinsack seriously furrowed by
time, genitals soft and enlarged from years of use & praktike,
what if we be praised for the largesse of our vaginas! the up-
right lengthening of our clits! the weight of our brestes! we
can flap large as pelicans our span as powerful as mythical
wings! can lose armies in our folds! and foronce forever be
praised for the duration of our satisfaction! can go round
oclock with the right caresses, our pleasures large with ex-

perience opens the secret to many sutras, drives many complexes ore'-boord and away, and what if we be praised for once forever for the loudnesse of our orgasms! as contagious as yawning or laughing, they have been known favouren the cycle of the moone, favouren tidal changes. The day is icumen in appreciation of our aliveness, you awaken to the wild richenes of your own true being, and we will shower you with mo cosmic seedmilk than you eva dreamed of!

Rosa mundi

Some will objeck what I dispute my allocated seat at the end of the long table, the truly veray long table. Or find obscene what I propose to speechen bout ma lifes slow climb in nottygrotty details. Adventure makes aventure wiser. Betcham making fy of hierarkies! & genealogiks! Wont suffre any ranking no mo nor be placed at the bottom of mine pile nor of any kinds Noway Isay, you can clepe your English rose, am the rosa Mundi, #mytime #is #nou #! Stand out shape stirrers, love-warriors, thinkers of the sphere, rosas immoveable, wise bovine guerillas-of-the-square!

I telle yous

Nodout some of you will ridicule my holistic cosmological views on mariage, dynamic unions, venus and jupiter, love, passion & justice, the importance of transmigration, tree-hugging & anniesprinkling. I used to have a mo urban pragmatik view on this whats for certeyn, but I like to think I move with the times. As agenders change and the oceans rise and the citees sprawl, mariage needs be large! accountable! not reserved for the benefits of one, needs revise its views on ownership & burghery. And domestick bliss! Needs provide a betre ensample for the ensemble! Let folks of alle gendres creeds coloures and sexes, esp. those what know best what it feels like to be owned and belittled by isolated servitude or preachers rules letem meet & mete in strengthened unions. And create new transactions. Nat settlen playen bride! alwayes remember you are who you be, lead the charge of change the deep deep change!

Despite much suffering past and to come for siker, I telle yous, we knead put all oure efforts in the long battle for fair share for alle, good chiere, reach for new emotions, strong nerve, all what needs calculating and dividing allrounde into

smalere shares, new homings, composite tribes of multi gen-
eracioun & originacioun. Workidout, not time awasting, lets
follow pleasures instrument resonators, the frictions of jus-
tice, oure beings engaged in the futures urgent makinges of
love!

Yoni

Searching ma body I objected it to various kinds of aerobics
wrappin ma yoga round ma neck nat ulikt a goose a swan or
a cran strakt to crane. Certes ma neck thus stretched nat ulikt
a common hern or heron or powerful cormeraunt low flying
oshuncatcher wat straunge flemengo is the sacred ibis the
ancient & the recent egrets. Ma throat thus wrapde to limit
around itself twisted tightly, bad air came out this side ma
knot & that side ma nus, what smelly bestiary is unhinged,
what stream of forgotten forgetting what knew bare bonds
about move into muscle focus & stretch ma resolve. This
shackle sbeen warping ma fitness! Th animal's in me, think-
ing groing learning pumping ma bumcheeks to breastbuns
mental concentrate much improved. Soon can chillax ma ef-
forts, sofen up wid ointments, get ywaxed all over, mead and
prepare for all those what will be precious, nodout make me
trouly.

Somme me founde 2 sexy, and som 2 saucy, and som 2
spicy, and som 2 chatty, and som 2 dizzy, and som 2 loude.
Like a maiden touched for the veray firest time som me
founde real HOT!

1DJ2MANY

Get ur freak on, lickes Misdemeanor
Don't try 2 fight it
Put on that dress I'm going out dancing
starting off red clean and sparkling
Saturday Night's alright if you put it on
I've been watching you (the way you move your sexy bodey)
Ain't nobody makes me feel this way!
Do I move you, are you willing
Do I groove you is it thrilling?
I don't want to move too fast, but cant resist your sexy ass
Wont you please let me lay you down
Take me down to your river
I wanna get free with you
Baby my heart's full of desire and love for you
Pull up to the bumper baby and drive it in between
This is the Good Stuff

Oooh

It's so good, it's so good

Love me that's right

Wanting . . . needing . . . waiting

Ooh ahh

Sock it 2 me like you want to ooh

My hormones jumpin like a dis-co

Love to love you baby

You can ring my bell, ring my bell

Just cant get you out of my head

Can you feel this beat, it's an obsessive heartbeat

Fever in the morning

Fever all through the night

Baby let me be your fantasy

Baby this constant craving

You're so soft you make me hard

Honey honey, don't conceal it

I'm so excited I just cant hide it

Soothe me I want some suga in my bowl

The way you smell can we go there

My milkshake brings the boys to the yard

Do your thing

A pretty girl in her underwear

If there's anything better in this world who cares

Upside down

Boy you turn me

Inside out

And round

and round

You can slide slide

Slippity slide

I, how u say, I wonder u, I wonder u

Oh ma lou oh ma lou oh marilou

So slide a bit closer to me little girl

See daddy's on a mission to please

Be my girl BoogieChild BadMan BabyGirl HotBoyz Oh

Sinnerman SupaFly SupaDupaFly Loverboy Lovertits

LilStar

Oh my Lover

I'm not a woman

I'm not a man

I'm something you cant comprehend

I am a threshold yearning to sing

Partly fish, partly porpoise, partly baby sperm whale,

Day and night, night and day, why is it so

One hand allows the other

I'm in the sky when I'm on the floor

Desire is hunger is the fire I breathe,

love is a banquet on which we feed

Star power star power star power over me

It's coming for me thro' the trees

I love visions of you endlessly

I just want to scream to the sky

It's a wild celebration of feelings inside

Fall with me for a million days

My sweet waterfall

Into my arms oh lord, at last my love has come along

And the moon and stars were the gifts you gave

It's simply beautiful

You can feel it in the air

All is full of love

Breathe to the rhythm

Dance to the rhythm

Work to the rhythm

Live to the rhythm
Love to the rhythm
Slave to the rhythm
Like the surge of a wave
and me the naked island
I love you I love you
Oh yes I love you
(me neither)

Wanhope

Baby light ma fire! A thousande songs preparen a thousande nights of true lovin'. Yit desires also a treacherous mysterious matter can uptrip one into very unexpected & daungerous habitats, bedeviled in disguise, & ruin ones already very temporary life with just misaligned rubdouns or a tricky kiss. Like consorting with a shutdoun or fearful or needy lover can greatly reduce the mental freedam of any growing intimatee and even end upcalling mental dragons emotional reruns from once own deep. Get one stuck instead for years from slowly sinking joye to swamplands of wanhope ensom despair.

The poor wretch tale

Witness straunge tales like the paur wretch who said they heard her disapproving mothre every team she cussed hire beloved. Unable to control the impack of that hungry gost on hire intimasee, she were left unceremoniously oon rainfulle morninge when the beleaving outwent for a pack of cigarette fags.

Saintly Catherine

Next time knowing betre given the various motivations of ma previous owned unions, wise & patient about love will I aim to be, even obedient with love, heeding Saintly Catherine. Let desire opene the soul like 'tis a belle chose. Let only a veray true being present vemselves what best shows promise to pleasen & easen, to caren & exploren, while allowing hemselves to be loved & opened & enrobed by the living giving wetness of ma heorte and of ma cunte, quod thoughtfully Alisoun.

Pop

Meantime biding ma time I pop horny capsules, chose ma membre sola cording to the hete of ma moode, be it in lethre wood bronze or jade, pump caress through series of vibrations from lang to short and cwick then staccato, arching ma back until I offgete oooh with oon loude sigh liquefy ma vrgent need into the warmste layzieste pools! Ma minde so satisfied spille its chemistry in the mostest fertile psychedelich of landscapes, and falle to schlep I do on a bed of dandelions parachuting in the winde. Houres later, stirred by revellers, I awake from my dram, still wet and ready to go. And off we'll went! raving into the strawberry fields with lectric ladies, fascinating boys.

Morning star

We'll party 'til the morning ahora, 'til a lick of light through a nihturnal cloud of dust of seafoam of poisoned air signale a turn from owle to nittegale. And there she'll was! Stonding on a big scallopshell surrounded by small winged animals and gold droppings, surrounded by delicat introcat leaves from luscious perennials, like quince trees, almond or olive trees, overgrown raspberry blackberry bushes, she b tracing the orizon rounding the trees the briddis with threads of firegold, down to their fineste details, Venus shine brightly, make me see the morning star! She calls out oure crew! Mama girls and boys, make me see the world is alit with loves mischievers!

A cracking tale

All Summer long we dropped the love we dropped the love like runny eggs dropt out of our Box. Egg in the evening egg in the doorway drop one on the kitchen-table one in the oven egg on the bathmat egg on the mutt egg on the pedigree egg down a shot like a yello blink crack a liquid one in the files down the servers tween the pages of the better books egg on the bus seat egg down the pipes egg in the wallet egg down the line egg in the plugs rich yolky egg juice on evry card reader in the slots of evry ATMs egg over evry screen egg over evry street camra egg in dust particles and air particles running down streams & rivers egg in the linings & buttons of evry uniform egg in the lines of the holograms of bankcards passports ID-cards railcards. You name it throughout Summer we dropta love we dropta love. Love juice lifeyolk running sticking into evry figment imaginable!

Yolk music

Now our tongues swelt into red roosters genitals groine into large forests & rock arrangements quim feathered trumpets and winged cocks into careful jigsaws. Limbs turn the translucent wings of raw shrimps, treeshaped daphnes laurels escape the bark stars explode. Heavy breasted milk overflow the banks, our drunken thighs blow into the thighs of powerful satyrs free the spirit of atalanta, skin taut for loud entoning fill the baseline, w knowen & unkowing sounds, branches tune lyring lovestrings, our hairs are glued with omlets & mud & sweat, & glitring popsicles & insect scales, the trees smelt of sex & yolk & purpl blue! Pleasure collapsed the city the countryside the whole country, its release possesd us all, love raged screams rose from evry nook & cranny, reachd any dark forgotn alley any forbidden area, swampd all categories, hurrid along the birth of babies lambs rabbitlets, quickend the leavening of bread stoppd hiccuping short, drivers drove up the other way, tax offices sent back due sums soldiers dropd their weapons for a long hallucinogenic breather in open landscapes, & all sordid professions (politicians, bankers, lawyers, mediamoguls, webtycoons, judges, TV hosts, billionaires, et al) were flogged dry and disbanded, sent to their guantanamo, while gentle dying friendes, neighburghes and faderes did a final soaring. Som I'm told even left this rough plane, this shade of pale smiling, calling out for mo.

Caxton's eggs

There's another egg story I telle. Its the story of some merchants going down the Thames. In the preface to the Eneydos Caxton tells a story of some merchants going down the Thames. There was no wind so they landed on the Kent side of the river to buy food. And specyally he axyed after eggys. And he asked specifically for eggs. And the good wyf answerde that she coude speke no frenshe. And the good woman said that she spoke no French. And the marchaunt was angry for he also coude speke no frenshe but wold haue hadde egges. And the merchant got angry for he wasnt speaking no French and just wanted eggs. And she vnderstode hym not. She didn't get that. And thenne at laste a nother sayd that he wolde haue eyren. And then at last another said that he just wanted eggs. And the woman said that she understood hym well. And the womman got that.

'Loo, what sholde a man in thyse dayes now wryte: egges or eyren?"

As a translator of books which were to be printed in England, Caxton had to choose. 'Certaynly it is harde to playse euery man by cause of dyuersite and chaunge of langage'. Certainly 'tis hard to please evrybody cos of the city's dew and cooking of our language, seyde he.

Weder

A total solar eclipse came down plungin us in t darke. Soon after 11AM three celestial bodies in a straight line during a short path of totality, the lunar shadow passed over many towns and cities of Europe and Asia from the ground looking up wearing special filters many of us shadow-spotted round the fields had driven down from the cities to the fields to witness tha Diamond Ring. Just as the dark fell just when it got dark there was a quick chill amixed of arousal and palpable panic a clear chill as the light disappeared a cold rushed in *what if the light, what if the light*

Never did 30 secs seem so charged, silence so silent day so distant. Then a low beam of slow thick runny gold etched out the small of the orizon & the sun poured over everything.

Summary

That same seson cattle large and smale be slaughtered moosten by the hundred thousande, up e doun the countries for feeding them their own innards & speed up mass consumption, and the calves too and the sheppes too. The fields eerily grene empty with death convoys full of carcasses slaughterhouse down pumping rivers of blood. Under such bad alignments, a terrible unease perservered wherever we went that somer as did the weder. One would have hoped this would restore a balance but boilled chikenes come chlorinated instede now, and puppy love has come an industry of muchel new type of wastage.

Septembre

The month of Septembre was the hottest Setember on record. Octobre the hottest October and so was Novembre and so was Decembre, flowers bloomed until mid-october but they grew too quickly, released no scent and were prone to tortured desiccated shapes.

July

In the coldest July a very rare sighting had been spotted on a housing estate in Westminster the Kangaroo Apple native to south-eastern Australia a small and spectacular sub-tropical shrub with ornate purple flowers and red berry-like fruit had been thriving in the excessive London heat. While just days before Halloween Sun-bathers swarmed on Brighton beach.

Decembre

In the first days of December bumble bees that usually hibernate underground from April to September were still buzzing in the cooling urban haze & that weekend a tornado hit the Northern part of the city ploughing through rows of houses as it funneled the quiet residential streets.

A Whole Year

Our twisted entangled longing were like the weather travelled unevenly painfully across the nervous system, the kidneys, breathing in its microparticulates. For a whole year it followed us in this way carving its tortuous demanding path

within us spreading political disorder blooming in English,
backyards thrown to sea mid-January kids knifed down
borders secured snow, unable to settle in Stockholm crowds
beached at immigration humback trillionaires in power news
of earthquakes at work on set disastrous floods in offices
raped healthcare annuled endangered hospital shutdown
nightingale iceberg migration in newly deforested bitches
personnel in Asia fracking in Cardiff for lack of foreign
whales continent after continent domino after domino
catching fire and drowning at one and the same time, in Cali-
fornia in Malaysia in Southern Iberia catching fire drowning
choking shot immense bladders of seals full of plastic beaches
catching fire.

Bookes

Ye know, books used to be me forbidden continue Alisoon. And writing hem unfinkable. Some things best wemmen nonderstanden, affirmed Juvenal or was that Furnivall, language at our disposition cropped back to a minimum for fear I mighty speke, like Eve did who spoke, St Bernard sayn, but once and threw the world into disorder. Even Dame Christine din piss about & wielded some stronges wordes for which she be seriously taskt & ridiculed for centries. Books, or bokes or bookes as we called them then were used to keep chicks & outher menial birds on the farm down, like Joan ne sheep & they burn small fry & odires are stoned while armies of clerics still cuss us with their höly bök.

Bookends

Certes y wet wool I used to be physically beaten with large voluminous leather bound to the bed while manly folks would

read and balk by the fire at the succubines what fill their pages
& agree Pardee the sexual life of bitches sure is a dark conti-
nent for psychologie, this stuffs been filling their pages ever
since! Ndeedy todays mother-hating scribes squeeze old
sham out of the same greased up postules just different spelt
& tweet nomynously to shutup me schlarly Beard. Not spare
me deaf threats of torture disembowling stoning rape or any
similar sort of gentilese.

'N fact will happily give the boote to the Abbott MP even
shoot up that good apple Jo Cox MP to her untimely grave.
Murder by design kepen ous all at home & mostest of all,
docile, obediente and

QWYETE

Bygod, if femen hadde written stories like those clerkes
have withinne hire oratories they wolde have ritten of men
moore wikkednesse than al the mark of Adam may redresse!

So what's the use of more books if they don't fight back?
Give me Patti Piss Factory Smith!
Give me the Slim Lady real Slim Lady Jordan!
I'm unspeakable Acker!
Just call me Castor! Mongrel! Zami! Outrider!

Call on the Butlers when u need one:

the one carrying the clear parables

the one carrying the opaque entities

Not spare me the SCUM

How deep shall we dig, Arundhati

What scribe Lispector digs up infrastructural hurts

With eyes so used to darkness as ours

Call up the Citizen and their Waterfall

O Cidadan! O Cadoiro!

There is no half measure Loy

Stay with the trouble! Let them eat chaos!

They say that, the women I love, they say:

I've tried to tell of a world that doesnt exist to make IT exist

They say that they foster disorder in all its forms

the femaled the misfits the misloved the uglies the oldies the

losers the foundlings the kingkonged

they say that

I began to speak.

Words I had never heard myself utter before came pouring

forth

they say that

Freedom is a constant struggle

they say that

the need to forget pain but not its origin

they say that

we call combat: the sensation of acknowledging one's own

emotions

they say that

It's always too soon to go home

Create what nourishes trust.

who namoore axe

how to spell YNOGH

than how to spell

AMOR

Can you see can you see can you see

They jus open their pages wide

and Audree Lordee, they give a good affront!

who wrote SILENCE WILL NOT PROTECT YOU

who kenow how to use books

making me sing

in jaguar harmonics

singe the Fast Speaking One

making me sing

when all language is migrant

making me sing

Caged Bird singing

& they dress so fine n they look so good

Soul stirring with their wordes

rousing millions of ones

to turnen their life

& maken a room of ones own

turn the page & get up!

pull a scroll

out of your interior

turn the page & get on!

turn your page & get out!

It's like ha said, slim Lady, from now on

I COMMIT MY BODY & MY LANGUAGE!

Hélène

Well I had a body yet I was with the dead, quod Hélène. ON POUVAIT ME FAIRE MAL À LA LETTRE I could be hurt down to the letter, writ Cixous. You wont kill you'll be killed. You wont write you wont touch, those are the laws of the foreigner. I had no roots no legit language yet I adored, and adoring came I to.

Fnesen

And then I fnesed, inks anothe scribbla, and something hap-
pened.

I fnesed n sneezed n somethink else beginned, besneezed be-
crossed ma death with ma life, she penned. Upcame for aire,
broke thru the lake. Sneezed and awaked strung up like the
strings of a lyre.

Sneezed and waked up as a whelpe, waked up a tyger waked
up as an elephant a bear.

Waked up as a fighter a grr-l a feral animal.

Waked up burning from unhealed wounds inflicted over long
stretches of torment.

Waked up singing.

Waked up a survivor of ruins a collector of moments

a space-time traveller a collective speecher a revolutionary.

Upwaked a rowdy lover an ancient teacher a spinner of
threads.

In the dream of it all, upwaked to visions of baboons & saints,
crowds & herbs.

Upwaked carried, protected & spoken for

by many hearts and hands.

Waked up with sharing & well-being as oures rallying weapon

oures communal invite, oures commons!

Waked up as an alisoun, nothink to scare me off now!

its about gossipes and learning

ystanding stead in godd companye, riding it despite circum-

flexiouns, sofening ma seat to

deepen the ride.

Aye, 'tis a simple thingy, how sneezing & hurting & riding &

sofening can change ones life

Midfinger

And to all those who ignored me and ma multiple kinds and

the rich persisting fruits of our beings labure, kept us vexed

in the anteroom for as long as possible, not easily led through

to next levels of influence, gotta prove many points, display

much talent and skills, but not too much, no thats too much,

and just a few of us at the time, no thats too many, well ma

expletives combust the paper of yo dictionaries, while funke

you too! we're in the scrolles in the folios in th archives in the

maginaries in the geologies of langages whats where we go,

shapeshiftynge many grotesqueries, partaking mythmaking

devising of depe renewall depe structural change, wave after

wave, gen after gen, enough to finally stick it. Create it word by word line by line book by book knowing by knowing radically differente ngineering of our lives. Change layer by layer, lie by lie, fear by fear the imprint of future conditioning applied bestest fruitfully to alle aliking.

Breathing

"Another world is not only possible" responde punditctivist Arundhati, "she is on her way. On a quiet day I can hear her breathing".

Rodney

Tis like what piece by what gr8 artist & goode gossibe Rodney McMillian who sows seams to see what seems to keep things the way they not sposed to be. Hisse black shiny vinyl landscape of black textile erectiles on white walls in white artworld sown up allrounde with white thread, whats a great piece of work! and series of workes, bruised and angry yet always seductive & sexual. Intimately politikal, and whats where the anger comes from: dealing with the truth while still being stitched up:

What yow see: black or white?

I see red!

Spero

Right on! xlaims what artist Nancy Spero, I've copied out re-
ports hung them on the gallery walls for all to see the terror
and the torture, rape by numbers, rape by camps, sometimes
copying typing out stamping quoting taking on, still making
work out of clean-ups like a Ligon, like a Lacy, carrying in
ones body the burden of otheres pain, otheres codex skin as
ones work, kepen each truthe each testament alive, relived
individually recorporated testified & geloved like a Piper a
Hiller a Boltanski, docu leaking body leaking holding on to
proof & dataflow in an age that chastises, isolates what it de-
bases, turns into mass what it depersonalises. Whissle n blow
into structures of lies ma heroes! like a red-haired Chelsea
Manning or an Ed Snowden or a calm Summer-dressed
Leshia Evans or a probing Carol Cadwalladr. Each holden
their owned prescious life for truf & the dearlyfe of all.

Accessory

And don't forget the textbook! exclaims the historian. If we're
not in the textbook all efforts are like swimming upstream.
For what's the best accessory? acquiesces the fashion de-
signer, but a book.

Schoo

Btw kindly please, quod Ali, ne want seme rude, and well mighty be wrung bout this. But on 1st impressions please let what weedy poet, Vallberg or outhere, letta nat not represent me maselfe and I. Forshoo means well but wont go the whole hag! 2 bloody well-educated makes her circumflexed all these bookes read n written n still nit nat not finisshe here sentences! She nat have a big front, simpel. Far 2 creepers by privilege & history, encumbered by heartbreaks to maken the total moostest of hire goode gelucke & lete others too benefiten! Meanit, beforen ich letta her speeche and gramatise ma name, let her dig deepe, knees deepa, worke harde faste at steppen outta hire selfes. B4 I letta kisse ma uilty plaisirs, ma bow sneakers, ma mesh-cnit chunky Guccis, ma golden metallic Nike Air Max 97 Special Ed or even ma Vivobarefoot a mostest simpel apperel for a nude lizardly look is the best for riding, firstly letta take mo risko! And then we will see her metal, for schoo.

Herte

*The text is in clear, well proportioned minuscules, with the words not di-
vided, the tails and tops of the letters of proper length, and the strokes of
the m and n inclined towards the left; graphic characters which indicate
the ninth century, and the kind of writing termed Caroline. Owing to its
manifold excellencies. The rapidity with which it could be written, the ease
with which it could be read, and economy of parchment, the Caroline min-
uscule, as it is usually called, grew rapidly in favour and finally became
the literary hand of all Western Europe,* acc. to OED.

Carolinian

Ah watchmam belle-ringer choir leader! It's not all of a piece!
Whamo I dont like to brag nor blow my own trompette but
let me remind you straight off the bat that a type of script is
named after me, which by way of ease and popularity in your
epoch therabouts would be pretty much like the invention of
ebooks and podcasts in mine. Might take awhile to manifest
but not negligible I'd say.

—

Now before I start my defence, before I start ma xcuseme, now that I finally can speech in my name sortov for a few kilobites, not scribe you down without an endin sight, I need a break, a pause, a short breather—

Thanks

And then, said I addressing Alisoun, then let me give thanks, show some gratitude, just in case I dont get to do it later on. Send some love and respect.

First I wanta thank you. For the opportunity. With the time-stretch of your audience that's major exposure of a deep cyclical nature and I need to live it down. Want to send my love and shoutouts to my favourite peeps, alive and unalive, my love and affection for shared life and care and growth, and all I never got to say. To my teachers and mentors, guides and healers, for the meanders behind and the road ahead who stuck by me, taught me one step at a time, one action at a time. Breakthroughed me, waxed pummeled and eased the fear out of me year in year out, massaged my heart and mind until I got it, or enuff of that to take the next and the next step for ma life. Much love to my friends, travel companions, blessyou for the thick and thins and pinks and blues of the uppers and downers, the details and the share-outs, big and small, we make family! who lent me your own torchlights, moved me forward when I was knocking about in the dark of my life, and for awhile there I was going nowhere fast, rowing in the same circles with one oar, you know who you are! and yes we're doing it.

My thanks to all youse near and far who showed me alleyways backstreets side-doors, unlatched maindoors, helped shape a route out of the stalemate, shifted my perspective on the significance of access and networks and influence.

And finally, to the seated figures, to the contemplative breath, sparks of light, grains of sand, to the ringing air, the bright prayer, the cold mornings, the large winds, and the floating mountains, blessyou as you make me, as you show me my size only to make me more profoundly sizeable—

Confessio

So now, Alisoun, to the matter on hand. For years I confess I believed all I was told and took it all upon myself. Thought that my vowels were too curly for grand plots, that my consonants were too elongated for effective ideas, that my continuity would be lost to my era, that pouting too much silly pressure on the palatial area had swelt my articulacy and made my telling totally unreadable, unsharable, certainly quite useless for any sort of more generalised activision or cultural service, that I was good for now but not for later, and needed to recognise when to bow out. That a female's cultural imprint is on a timer, a temporary quota. This had filled me with rage but didnt know how to upspeak, fly in the face, fight the battles while anchoring my anger, this had made me despondent, and for a time had paralysed me. Thyngges change. Now I dont care. Trust what I must. Sgot to be said, times a-not waiting, there's work to be done, worlds to be drummed out.

Mouthpiece

Damn Dame, you're not sure about me for a mouthpiece? Yes, dont answer that, I get that! There's lots of prouder speedier writers around that would make for betre less-burdened transporters. Still, I've given years to work in your shadow, even to be your shadow, your honest copyist. Locate your voice through me, in me, yet not for me. Is that what this is all about? At work's ende, will this in fact have changed my own voicing too? Tbh I've always felt we were a bit ill-matched. Looking for relevant ways to reinvest your iconic figure's speaking habits as the impressively loudmouthed past-future era maximalist female that you are has been a pretty taxing task for the troubled foibled comlicated 21st centry writer fighta that I be.

Panache

Yet you've become a trusted demanding presence. The inwit to my dimwit, you bully me, hurry me along. In the end I get it. The tenure of your skip, the purpose of your scat, the way I see it now, it's all about panache. The panache with which one deals with what one is served up. And how one dresses it up. Not to care about any whatswhat. Dust it off, live a life, pushing through it to make way for oneself and ones others. A figure like yours speaks to me. Encourages not a hide-out so much as a face to face. Like self-worth, what one gives to the fight, how far one is prepared to go. It's to do with one's active anchoring in the world, figuring out some of one's own hold-ups to this process, reaching and establishing a richer deeper awareness, more clarity and personal honesty. What personal symbols, what coping mechanisms, what excitements, or terrors, or fears from sense of duty, or of ingrained inadequacy have dictated my choices, what I stay with, what I pursue, what I abandon or veil. How deep I dare to go, how much I hold back and the reasons for this. No wonder youre on my case! masking and unmasking the masking.

Hungry Ghosts

No doubt my renewed urgency was also prompted by a continuous low-level nausea at the institutionalised violence, continuous abuse and disregard in all manners of degrees for all sorts of femaled and differential beings, even as histories differ it's all of a piece with xenophobico-misogyno-racisto-go-to-hell-o'type of wordlchew. Given the hate misery being pumped into the collective, the brutal unflinching numbering numbing down of our being, and of all beings, the preventing of peaceful mass demonstratings, replaced by the spewing of continuous low-level blue electric nausea, pulsating drones, make allround crazed, with schoolyard stabbings, FB murders, primal porn, self-loathing and scorn, abuse and disregard, applied in all manners of degrees to any sort of new conscience being, how it wildfires across social media, raises walls, isolates neighbours, graffitis shit and vomit on the doors, acid at bus stops, sloganeering that passes for language, insults for public speech, old modes of territorial injury come far too readily to hand, and given that its all of a piece with the worship of brute wealth, superiority complex, generalised corruption, the allowance for unthink-able levels of greed, the privatisation of the elements, ram-pant pollution, air poisoning in sprawling megamonstros-ities, microparticulates found all the way up the most distant mountains, the radical disappearance of bio- and linguistic diversity, overfishing, rising sea levels, et j'en passe! wed be forgiven for feeling totally overwhelmed and scrambling at this stage!

1:13

Or like the great Indian sage Shantideva said: "Just as by the fire that will destroy the world, Great sins are surely and at once consumed by it. . . . . For beings long to free themselves from misery, But misery itself they follow and pursue. They long for joy, but in their ignorance destroy it as they would their foe".

Fight

Today Alisouns of all genderings are kicking up a fight! from the darkest bowels of our time. How does one kick up this fight? With both slow and fast responses, both in large and micro scales. Through both contemplation and action. Through beauty and anger, dialogues dared initiated presented, high and low, cost what may, whatever time it takes, however many insults, incomprehensions, there's work to be done, writing to be writed, typing to be typed, voicings to be voiced. I care less so I care more. Total dedication and a clearing of one's intentions. Today just got started—

Outings

As for the goss of my life as a lover? The stories of my own pleasures and strifes? And what marriage counselling you might want to draw from these? Im sure you want the lowdown on that. Yes, you dont need to answer that. Now that I'm entering the prime of my life, I look back on my earliest adventures as though we were exploring houses or forests, ferreting, sniffing each other out, all of us alike aliking, alike about to differ, into girls and boys and all subtle variations on a scale, a blend of bods and worlds, some difficult to tell, some hesitant, not as yet scared off, something in each aroused and undoubting, whatever the way of the rub, go about it with stunned fever with fabulous kissing lips with bright eagerness opening their sexual folds after folds growing their pole all the way the sex to the throat their clits shiny and hard grow into branches into silver rivers leak milk from their breasts from their cock rubbing thighs riding hard bleeding a full month in cupped love-hand in locked embrace insideout heat on heat young and sweaty as we be, we were melted glass love's luminous malleable playthings!

Wetness

Found girls to be my favourite adventures. Lyrical, exploratory, togethered without a name nor genda at first for it, girls within girls, yet beyond girls or boys, aloved with wetness and daring energy and heart of femaleness wasall. Made my life with one two three of her, and for awhile we were very lucky in love. Ever moreso when after generations of struggle and sacrifice while still at times carrying the blight of fear at the shortness of my breath, or at the persistence of my silence, it was to be our good fortune our very good fortune to live to become full citizens, female citizens, queer citizens unioned in love and protected in law.

Two women

Yet I found these also to be the most soul-searching and diffi-
cult of adventures. In fact it seems I can't continue being your
scribe unless I mention for the record a most intense purging
of love. Went as far as losing any sense of the shape of my
heart, nor of my genitals, nor of the flowers along my spine,
nor my joy of travel, nor my independent mind and explora-
tory streak. It's a long story and there are many other com-
ponents and years and beings and losses arounding it. But in
short, we had ended up, she and I, our skins raw and in-
flamed, our hearts parched, at the two separate ends of an
ever-growing field of searing sorrows, angry wounds. From
here, distance cannot be breached and there is no way to cross
or come closer. We watched us burn until there was only
scorched earth and the cold light of day. Yet how we had
wished for growth together, fertile fields, homecoming! How
we planned and updreamed a life, two women with love, and
how painfully and ignorantly we had gone about it, misusing
all of our differences, Odi et amo.

Heloïse

What a saddening story, whispers an Heloïse, even as you sought the freedom to love, seems you unbuilt all your bridges, undid all your knowledges, misapplied your bestest experiential wisdom.

Ah, dear friend yes, and the world seems of no succour then as you well know, whispered I in reply. So please let me ask you, what is the point of intimate love? Beyond the lectric arousal of hormones and feelings, what is this great encounter? What is the naked truth of what it means to love and be loved, way inside and beyond genders, why to release and be released in such a way. And for what and why do we wade through the powerful marshes of pleasure and loneliness, desire and connection, often missing the point of such intense light and dark encounter, letting onself be drawn to the wrong lighthouse, only to end up pillaged pirated stranded on the beach and suffering extensive long-standing power outage?

Experience

Well, in ma experience, intercepts Alisoun. Nono, said I, please let me do this, my questions are my lessons and my stories, I've waited so long to gedit took so long to healit. For a few years, my soul was silent, aura crumpled down at my feet. As shocked as rows of ice-cubes in a blue freezebox. When the thawing began so in earnest did the loss. Impersonal, far bigger than I was. Neither woman nor man nor flowers nor the waves of the sea nor any kind of comfort could come near, nor ease this desolation. In a dark cloud I roamed prone to any passing hallucination like St Antony in his desert or Julian on a bad acid trip in Norwich. No shewings here but Fear who reared its ugly bottomless head and made me as shaky shivery as the hindlegs of a whippet. Yes, don't say anything.

Forms

These gendered sexualised forms that clothe and design our paths in life, did I even still have such a form to claim and for what purpose? When loveless forlorn where is the reassuring solidity of form? What identity goes beyond one's identities when all is lived and done, all has been suffered and lost, what is the connection the mission that such nakedness announces? What full presence will be asked of ones reconstituted form? And how does one trust and follow love's continued apprenticeship, accept its larger purpose on one's life? What erotic depths, what intimacy and nearness will this demand and enable? How far to go, how much further in such raw unknowing. How blinded before one might finally feel even just a flicker, a faintest heat of light far within one's being unravel the hold of form into patterns of breathing, heat oscillations, heart beat.

Pause

When I came to, I had just turned thirty-and-seven-thir-teen-and-aphew, and age was catching up. Now thats another surprise development that will push the buttons of any form of sexuality, identity and visibility!

Right on! exclaims one similarly challenged, menoing out, drenched in hydraproduction, seems to suffer the onset of a slow slumberous mind, intercut with crazy visions and re-bellions, chaotic ondoings, memory losses, fevered insom-nia, softening limbs, obviously shedding one comfortable skin and cruising-speed for the wilder unpredictable ranges of femaleness and wisdom ageing, while in the meantime, water running down the walls of her skin, she just glistens like a statue in the middle of a fountain.

Co-op

As for me, well, writes caroline, I have to concede that all the years of being bullied and harrassed, bitched about, and fighting with you, Alisoun, are bringing me back to my own time, slowly more grounded and available, full of a fighting spirit, more open and alive than before to surges of poly-morphous intuitions and processes of collective retribution, a necessary traumatised transition that rekindles intercon-nections, as much as tough, persistent cooperation. And I have come to realise that love is the calm available flowing in ones being. And it is this sense of right place and inner free-dom that by some happy streak might also lead one to stand in the path of someone, with whom pleasure and desire will burn bright and invite a desiring knowing. How to grow to be lovers for each other, with each other, and manifest as queerly beloveds in the world. Yes I reckon this is the closest I've come to understanding intimate love.

Lessen

The question arose about how to reintegrate a sense of myself. Not to give in to what one has lived through. Start moving towards new vistas without being lost to my lifes purpose.

How to find back to the ways of the heart. How to use trauma and sorrow. Not to settle at my initiatory identities nor any sort of behavourial fixity, rather move from anything that aims to hold me back in the narrows of one's known. Know it better, use it wiser. I tried to lessen the weight given to my bag of emotions. No longer be so easily tricked by fear, sadness, or even desire. Lessening their hold brought a sort of personal anonymity to one's experiences. I tried to decrease my attachment to one's perceived psychology and circumstances. All this opened up my life again, filled it with air and fluidity.

Parts

I looked for openings in the world. Let the ready or better parts of ones selves be given to landscapes, gatherings, inclusions, transmissions, translations. A spread of love. Let them rise and reach further. While the weaker parts must continue to heal and grow in dreamtime, and with healing, or medical treatment. I was going nowhere fast, what's for sure.

Training

When the worst was over, there was some travelling to be done. Meet people, histories, places, start to listen and learn differently, by following rather than analysing, sensing rather than drawing conclusions. I learnt how little I know of the world, yet how much of it is in the ways of the heart, or in one's willingness to let the heart continue the mind's training. This stretched my comfort zone, and my levels of honesty. I joined bands of scholars, healers, activists and travelling musicians.

Poetry

Reclaimed with the first that the arts of poetry truly have other borders than current temporary national languages. That poetry is connected to very different lingual, historical & transfugal streams. It is in that sense that it points to the future of all languages. And might fall out of favour for a time but when needed, at any epoch, will lead us back to breath, and to all the songs it carries.

Dialogues

From the others I learnt, painstakingly how to stay with the heart. Learnt what that might mean. But what is the heart?

The heart is the book, exclaim medieval lovers and philosophers. It is ones guidance and ones conscience hidden across inked out pages. It is the resonator chord, the *corda* of "hearts" when chanting, or when reciting by heart. I asked, is the heart guidance?

It is deep song, exclaims Garcia Lorca, the heart is duende. It is the shiver that traverses the ones who keeps the connections open, between blood, soil and song. It is the ancient force that courses the blood, the absolute belonging between soil and song, the dancer and their ground.

Ah but said Caroline, drifting, meddling, we mostly carry our songs in our bags in our jaws in our bones these days. Like tattooed roses, acquiesces Acker. Is this the heart: looking for the heart without losing heart? I asked. Is it to settle where one can & let one's dance mix in with the ground, writes Sara Ahmed. Sense its arrival routes criss-course the nervous system like the dowsing le Tout-Monde? Transforms the energy of love on the move, on the run? Is that the heart, I asked, a duende of mobility?

As a muscle the heart flows centrally to all animated life, yet like the soul in the pinky no-one knows where the rest of it really lodges. It is the feather that will weigh up the truth of your Gyptian soul at the end of your days. Is the heart empty to be filled? the emotion at a passing brush of air, or a whispered goodbye? Is the heart acceptance?

I asked, is it surrender like falling to one's knees, or sitting still in contemplation, surrender to the transformation of cyclical life, a grand scheme ready to be activated at the heart of now? Yet what is the energy the discipline the inspiration the humbleness that transforms this into love? Is it self-acceptance, discipline, compassion, courage that I seek? Is it the belly-laugh, the loud sigh of relief, the welling of tears when things click into place? is that the heart?

And what about anger? Harsh burning anger. Can this have heart or does that only occur once it has been transformed into something else, something purer, connected, elusive yet crystalline. Nearly sorrowful. Anger transformed into solitary sadness. Anger transformed into solidary courage.

Is the heart waiting for me to be ready? To breathe out and move out of cellular obsessions into activision, engaged intentions, is that the heart: the first blindseeing step one takes?

Then suddenly after years of searching, all windows flew
wide-open and I knew, that to be a poet is to be a bridge, to
be a lover is to be a bridge, to be alive is to be a bridge, to be
a fighter is to be a bridge, to be a caroline is to be a bridge.
To build bridges is to go all out, ride oneself out completely,
and be ridden so completely that it will hit a point of dissol-
ution and doing so, finds the new shorelines, flows with the
heart's currents, fills ones entire life present past and future
with truth, the truth of ones life's purpose. Thus it is guided
by radical negotiations of "love" and "self" and "you" that an
arduous lesson was felt. And a whole new cycle could begun,
more impersonal and regendered than before, clarere about
the lessons and demands of love's worldly embrace—

dream#1

I dreamed that first I must receive a body. It was a strange
dream with limbs hanging off hooks and heads with wide eyes
dancing off threads in vast blue aerated structures, like cool-
ing rooms. Someone is seated at the end of the rooms who
waves at me to come closer. She tells one, first you must re-
ceive a body. I am invited into it, invited to have one. To piece
one together. In dream one steps into this, one puts it to-
gether & become body. But this body has a mind of its own.

It bows and bends and kneels and lays down on the cold stones. It wants to lay itself down in front of her. One lays the full length of this body in front of her. One lays this body down in front of her, lay it down so deep one forgets how to rise. Lay it down deeply. Lay down deeply. This is how the thought in the dream went. I was invited to lay a body down until she invited me to rise.

dream#4

I stumbled on a pin. Not one pin. Rows and rows of pins. They pin-cushion my limbs like the limbs of beasts, decorate their necks, run in persistent and luminous fur-like waves around the bodies, refract light, like forms of healing that puncture the skin to revitalise blocked energy lines, and announce other states of form. Molecular patterns rather than figures, structural flow rather than arrested movement. Within separate apparitions and timelines, the luminous connectors.

dream#16

I came upon a very large red cabbage. It was lying head up on the ground. There was wilderness. On closer examination it turned round that it wasn't a cabbage at all but rather a large red-arsed aroused baboon. She was gorgeous. There was blossoming & a hefty struggle. Wide open to the waist in luminal flow. Scented juices sprouting from all fours.

dream#7

A thousand arms a thousand heads all around us in all registers like a noisy parliament. How many heads how many limbs a garland of skulls body sketches conscious unguarded pleasure the air was intoxicated with oils with drums silvery dancers frictions firing mind tremors a thousand dances shiva slipping from one shape to one shape multiplying into ten thousand shapes then ten thousand more kissing rubbing kicking biting perspiring entering exiting expiring loudly inhaling.

dream#34

Death is a relief but I enter it shamefully. I dream that death is a relief that I enter shamefully, having not realised my deeper self, forever caught in doubt while alive. In the dream one wakes up feeling one has died without realisation and through one's own fault, not through accidents or lack of support. There is a deep warning in many similar dreams about one's own death and dying. Not entirely sure what they are warnings about. Choices made or choices about to be made?

dream#27

I dreamed that someone, ancient, imagined or lived, chose me to be their carrier, their towncrier, and over time allowed me to recognise myself in them, looks like me, reflect myself in their image and projection and strengthen my dedication, work and practices.

dream #∞

Many times lately I dream that I can feel that I am held—

What do such dreams mean? They mean that the body's immensity absorbs its traumas into dreamtime. They mean that it is another history we dream of in these ecstatic forms, and that collected hearts will be carried by fearless and freed forms of love. Or nothing will be carried on at all.

So, anyway, said I turning to Alisoun, in the failing light of an evening, like I said, just use me, I can type, I'm on course, I'm onit.

Interlude

Lord Crist in Heavenes how changed your art! Xlaims Alisoun, taken aback ylaughing, obviously delighted with ma tirade, suddenly pleased at the prospeck of the good gossib she mighty find in me despite her worst fears. Yes ndeed you kisse ma botes deare! yes you ride ma pony, you creme ma lippes with your wordes and your time, forshure you nat be an Alisoun xactlye, but a kindred knihtly dame forshure not for show, that you art, that you be!

This remark coming as it did from a voice I had tried for years to maintain contact with, now hearing it spiral across epochs and solar systems to finally land in my corner, gave me such a rush that it nearly brought tears to my eyes. I decided to stop recording our song for a few days and outwent for a walk in the unkende widopened terrain my life had suddenly become. Her voice still ringing in my tympanye.

A figure takes hold. A figure is cut. Finds ground. Creases its grounding from ancient grounds. Travels like wildfire into the synaspses of the brain. Asks for my face to hold it between their hands. Dream-like shapes take over my steps, unfold in front of me as I walk.

Stitch

Word

Phewy! Sgot to be said your storytelling skills have moved me
deeplie! reprises the dame relieved to finally get a word in.
Youre pretty longwinded and spend much time beating yr-
selfe up, time is precious and yos a bit mismanaged, but you
get there I can see it nou. Me piache your persistance, your
intense process of betterment, even your candour has me got
encouraged.

Cloak

Recalling the bravery of all sistaspirit werreours, I get to cut-
ting & sowing from the fabric of your wordes and the tissues
of all our actions, a large bum, anglomaniac like a rebelllious
T made of local hemp. Without further ado I take to cladden
ma shape into uncompromised thoughts, right spectacle, not
elegant. Undercutting elegance. No fine line here, but a net-

work! can trace it all way back to the sheep's back in every faire of Englond. Or to the camels what come the longe rode round to Ghent im Flanders, heer forth truly the besteste markete! Asymmetrical clunky, exaggerated baroque shapes of bio-morphic features. Grene is the new rede, all natural dyes, and precious threadings, like we like to do back hem in my dark ages.

Threads

Ah but never as dark as yours, quod she interrupting her telling.

Looks straight at me with sudden pitié. In that instant, in that strange look, it is like mountains of time start to slide down between us like sand-dunes. A deep shiver shoots through the air, the veil trembles. I can feel she's only a few layers away, can sense her stirring excitement, the butterflies in her belly fluttring in mine. My skin lifts from me, turns into a structure of translucent threads. Afraid of disturbing anything, I stretch out as delicately as I know how. And stay afloat. Like a lit spider's web in the air. Amidst the weave. Can see myself sitting at this desk. Everything is muffled and weightless. It's so trippy, I feel dizzy. Then it's gone. My ears pop. Slowly I come back to my shoulders my neck my hands, stiff from the work, and a lingering tension, the clickety tap of the keys, traffic outside my window. And her voice in my noise.

Charge

Indeed, she says, if it werent for your uncontrollable reliance on artificial light, a lightbulb in every object, old batteries bleeding, electronic circuitry flashing from every corner, every little plug shines out of every seam and scam, makes your bodies dangerously over-charged, poisoned, heavy metal. And basically you're keeping the night so totally at bay, and with it the necessary counsel of sleep, dream and visitations, that if it weren't for that constant flattening led light sightblinding you, you'd realise you're even more in the dark than we ever were, pardi!

Fibres

Find me collaging each body shape, dreaming up my walkon, each a collectively combined modular garment of rhinestone, transeasonal tartans, honeycombed reversibles, rows of pins, waterproven with local linseed oile, pleasingly resuited, estranging from emprisoning habits, always knowing how slowe processes of change be. A genderending opulence up-dressed in fineste woodpulp & composted fibres. Flaunting ma fantastical natomical is an imaginary none has seen becoming. For revoluciouning one moostest dressen the part! From genitalie to lingerie to grouperie to co-created networks of designerie 'tis all one. Dame Vivienne calls it "seducing into revolt". No knickers to the crowning ball. Virginia Woolf called it "frock consciousness" reminds me a good friend over a fruhstuck of seeds and froytes, by which she meant the new found autonomy of corset-free frocks and androgynous breeches.

C.W.E.E.N

HERE COMES THE CWEEN. Dame LaWest, a designing quim so FIERcE & CONtrarian. S/he was dresd head2heels in a dappr dupr cOMBo o'BLK synth satn robe biodegraded beLO the kNee ycarryng a granbaby all-teed up "I am not a terrorist" ywrapd all faded GB flag for carDIGn mother-funken, still 2 kool for old skool th' ole muff!

Birth of Fashion

All excited for this latest brouha I ride into toun, dressed 2 impress, and to address, unhomed yet homely, xquisitely threaded in fabricated artisanry, outspoken craftivision is a strong sexualised co-dividual anarchism, "we are all feminists!" Then I go for the biggest shock of mine own time. A single bolt of fabric! Squares and rectangles! All in one piece! That is the pret ma medieval time gave to the birth of fashion! I return to it you now! a great blowe to industry, politicking, hypocrisy! We needs take fashion back to ma roots, from bloated need to bare care is a full on transformational design on global wear!

A Little Brun Dresse

How I hear you, quips the artist, mother, neighbour, jardener, voter, planner, sewing machine operator Alex Martin in positive acquiescence. For one year ma main outfit will be a single brown dress. Will wear only recycled accessories, like Stephanies one-niht stand recyclic tilettoes.

Th' aim is abstinence fro shopping, consuming, womaning, fashioning for one year. Might turn into tweye. Rethink in smale larger ways the whole design industry. And what one really needs. "Keep and Share" not fake needs.

Emma

Indeed, "we are in need of unhampered growth out of old traditions and habits" wrote Emma who kenew a thing or two about this kind of fing. Rebel Woman thrown out of countries left to right and back for bringing the future too closely. Textile factory is the seat of all revolution, quod she, wafting and weaving, all thinking and learning. Organising and actioning starts here. Don't axe, quod she, dig in! represent! Arise from superstition. Dance dance dance to the disarrangement. Come comrades la transnationale! Eg jeg ik en jeu in play. Jump ship mid-sentence & back. Take any fpigment wid you! Don't axe, slam bam, represent!

Brand

What plentifull stories telle ma opulent figure! tinues Ali. Each more becoming thanne each. Sayso meselfe maturity has me ageing like bran & rich fields of hemp into a whoole exciting array of multifunctional attributes & shapely designables. What is fashionable mighte not suit ma shapes, but what passes for fashion only cuts to size zero, and the label includes cold wash, and distant child labure, am a Lady not a stick! nor a prick! Ma folds from ma time lookie to the future, new materials from local trade, thinktank manufacture, homegrown glocal materials, retrain digital to material, height arts down to wearable crafts, organics and vegetable wear from syntheticks in regrown industry. Much recreation w/ design gossibes. How y rethink materials, provenance, all sweating politics associated with cloth and specific materials, n still look good to feel good! 'S muchel more to it bviouslye. A whoolye industry to change the ways we clad and clothe, stitch and dream. And in this, as in so many othere things I intente showe the way. You are what you are making! acquiesce poeta ctivist Anne Waldman finely bedressed outrider.

Thoreau

"I cannot believe" gloses the Hermit in the forest presciently "that our factory system is the best mode by which men may get clothing. The condition of the operatives is becoming every day more like that of the English; and it cannot be wondered at, since, as far as I have heard or observed, the principal object is, not that mankind may be well and honestly clad, but, unquestionably, that corporations may be enriched".

Tee

Yes, well, like, you probably need to be naked to read this paragraph with a clear conscience!" nterupts one fashionisto Thacara. Cos 700 gallons of freshwater have ingone make ma cotton Tee. Forfact a tee like mine is the reasoning why 85% of the Aral Sea in Uzbekitsan has disappeared. Water is used to grow cotton in desert and ¼ all insecticides in world are on cotton crops. Fashion accounts for 25% of the world's polluants. But whatodo?

Worne

Whatodo, axe yow? clips Alisoun, well no xpurt bviously, but have cut a few and have always liked well-worne. Well-worne worne well. Methink whats the clue. Well-worne attire ywearing well: a sign of good craftsmanship. The key is mo of less. Wear and wear. Glocalisation not globalisation. Small scaled production. Reclaimed yarn and re-knitting projects. Lowdown methink is slow. Slow slow slow. Slow slow slow slow slow slow slow.

Is the keyword slow now?! exlaims one merchant, makes no sense atall who xpecks no rewards unless mo mo mo! most think in millions, bigga betta pushing budgets whats the way.

More of less?! xlaims another, pologies but coming from you whats quite a surprising!

Slo

Ah no! there's no contraduction, responde Alisoun. Whamo a slow pace not prevents a large mindset. On the con'try like ping and pong and yin and yan and warp and weft what goes together dances to gather a quickening riverbend not preclude an ampling estuary, a fast downer not preclude a chillaxed climb, a quick lick does not preclude an unstoppable playsir or even a chain of playsures.

Slow is what will keep the world go round. Slow is a turn to a more post-industrial pre-calyptic pace of industry. Ma kind of time. Active not nostalgic. Functional not profit driven. But hurry to get there! Slow is the future. Or theres no future time at alle, simpel. Make slow clooth like there is slo food, slo local, slo mo, slo travel, slo horses, slo love, slo cookery, slo sieste. Slo Slow is the future or no future at alle, outshouts the medieval dame agitating.

Samples of action

Here followe some samples you mighty well finde valuable. Certainly can helpen choose ones coloures in the morning in the evening on matching or marching days. Whamo like Lucy + Jorge Orta who devise clothes what call survival and community gear, portable minimum habitats bridging architecture and dress can help reimagine social links. Or the storytelling video headgear by artgineer Krysztof Wodiczko worn by new arrivants to stop and share, a slowing device, a portunity for chat and care. Stitches weave stories that can save lives, Respect Philomena. The belowe is ne in no way exhaustible but hope it can helpe you fabricate the once you nede. Prepare for long days and nihts. Wear what says it all. Clothe your resistance.

Black

In January 1988, one month after the first Palestinian Intifada broke out, a small group of Israeli and Palestinian women stood once a week, at the same hour and at the same location—a major traffic intersection in Israel. They were dressed in black and held up a black sign in the shape of a hand with "Stop the Occupation" written in white.

Black

Between 1976 and 1983 in Argentina, thousands of people dissidents and civilians were arrested and vanished without a trace, taken off the streets, from their homes at night, or from their workplace in broad daylight. Dressed in black, The Madres de la Plaza de Mayo have been demonstrating for years every Thursday at 3:30 pm demanding to know the fates of their loved ones.

Black

Women's Aid to Former Yugoslavia was set up in 1992 to give practical aid and support to women on all sides of the Yugoslav conflict. Some of these women adopted the name Women in Black for non-violent direct action in the UK against militarism and war.

Orange

"Along with our allies at the lingerie designers Agent Provocateur, we developed a line of intimate apparel in Guantánamo orange, with "Fair Trial My Arse" emblazoned across the derrière . . . annnounced the director of Reprieve, the London-based legal charity that represents dozens of Guantánamo detainees on 14 feb 2008.

Pink

Following the US election the previous November, the Pussyhat Project debuted during the Women's March in January. Spurred by Trump's leaked "grab her by the pussy" locker room talk millions around the world channeled their outrage into knitting pink beanies with pussycat-like ears to "reclaim the term as a means of empowerment," as founders Krista Suh and Jayna Zweiman explained.

Red

The protest of a group of Latina girls on the steps of a town hall in Texas, who stood wearing their traditional *quinceañera* 15th-birthday gowns and sashes, drawing worldwide attention to Donald Trump's ruthless deportation legislation. Other young women have haunted American senate buildings where anti-abortion legislation is being heard, filing in silently to occupy empty rows of seats dressed in the red robes and white bonnets of *The Handmaid's Tale*.

White

Christina Broom, considered Fleet Street's first woman photographer, documented marches of thousands of suffragists and suffragettes wearing white dresses designed to prove to the country the dignity of their cause.

Yellow

Catalans wearing yellow shirts are forced to bin them before they can enter a football match.

Skin

A collective of older women farmers in Uganda stripped down in 2015 to protest loss of land in front of a huge gathering. On April 14, a group of elderly women stripped before a huge gathering called over a government plan to re-demarcate land for a national game park in Apaa village, Labala parish, in Pabbo Sub-county, Amuru District. Government officials had travelled there to explain that the government did not plan to take land away from the poor people. Gen. Aronda and many in the crowd focused their gaze away from Amuru women's naked power.

Skin

Russian protest punk group Pussy Riot are as famous for their use of the naked female body as they are for their colorful balaclavas, and Ukrainian protest group FEMEN often scrawl slogans on their naked bodies to speak out about sexism, censorship and objectification of women.

Lips

The tale of the textile workers who sewed their lips together in protest at inhumane degrading working conditions. The tale of artist David Wojnarowicz who sewed his lips togethre in protest at the silence and demonization arounding AIDS.

Beret

Symbol of the Black Panthers political organisation, initially Black Panther Party for Self-Defense, called for armed defence against racism and white imperialism. One of the more significant flanks of the Civil Rights Movement, 1950s–60s. Beyoncé's Angela Davis beret and army of feminist dancers channeled it at the Super Bowl 2016 in support of the Black Lives Matter movement.

Button

By the middle of the 1300s buttons were big business and people loved them. Tailors produced garments with row upon row of buttons with matching buttonholes. The word button appeared at around this time and stems from either the French bouton for bud or bouter to push. The Guild produced beautiful buttons with great artistry, much to the delight of the aristocracy. The peasants, however, weren't allowed to join, even if they could afford it. The aristocracy passed laws to limit buttons permitted for common usage to thread- or cloth-covered buttons & the button became a status symbol.

Button

In 1520 reports tell of a meeting where King Francis I of France, his clothing bedecked with some 13,600 buttons, met King Henry VIII of England, similarly weighed down with buttons.

Button

The sudden wide use of buttons worried the authorities. A woman was denied wearing buttons cos no buttonholes.

Dashiki

During the 1960s, those that were part of the counterculture movement in the United States grew their hair long and wore loose, flowing clothes in opposition to the rigid uniforms of the US military and, by extension, the Vietnam War. African Americans adopted the dashiki—a traditional piece of clothing from West Africa—as a reclamation of stolen heritage.

Arabic Tee

Iraqi blogger Raed Jarrar was stopped by security officials at JFK Airport for wearing a Tee and was forced to change the shirt before boarding a JetBlue flight: You know, I asked him, "Well, what's unsafe about this shirt? What do you think it means?" And he didn't actually comment on what the shirt meant. He just asked me, "Isn't it in Arabic?"

Slogan Tee

In 2005, created T-shirts that read: "I am not a terrorist, please don't shoot me"—worn by her 2 year old grandchild.

Silk

Was attempted banned by French Theologian 12thC for wearing worms' excrement (silk) and gold-embroidered edges.

Medieval fabrics

Medieval sumptuary laws regulate fabrics utilised in clothing according to social status. Across Europe. Regulate shape, size, class, wear.

Yarn

Craftivism in the US is largely associated with the resurgent feminist movement, but its roots trace back to colonial times. In the 1760s, women revolted against British taxation on textiles by spinning their own yarn and sewing their family's clothes. Famous spy Molly "Old Mom" Rinker smuggled messages to George Washington's troops through balls of yarn.

Quilt

A crowd-sourced quilt was first unfurled on the National Mall in Washington, DC. Comprised of thousands of lovingly hand-sewn panels commemorating lives lost in the AIDS epidemic, the Aids Memorial Quilt was an indelible example of hobby craft deployed for political protest, called "craftivism."

Sash

Between 1955 and 1994, the Black Sash provided widespread and visible proof of white resistance towards the apartheid system. Many members were vilified within their local white communities, and it was not unusual for women wearing the black sash to be physically attacked by supporters of apartheid. The Black Sash had many tactics to protest apartheid policies, one of which was "haunting" cabinet ministers with the silent presence of women wearing black sashes. Thery used to call it "haunting."

Cotton

Mahatma Ghandi and his followers were angered by the laws that sent local Indian cotton to Britain to be milled into cloth, and then sent back to India where the people were forced to purchase British loomed cotton rather than hand woven khadi. Gandhi saw the revival of local village economies as the key to India's spiritual and economic regeneration and he envisioned homespun khadi as the catalyst for economic independence. He built his strategy around the revival of traditional craftsmanship and skills that would feed local demand with local production, and encouraged the boycott of British goods, as part of policies of civil disobedience and non-cooperation.

Head

Once dressed top it all up. Much has been made of me cover-chief couerchief kouerchef keyrdchese the crimson twirl atop ma heed, continues Aly. Names me as it crowns me, this thing on my head is the passionate pulse at ma blood, the name I carry, the promise I most deliver. The beginning of ma voicing. Such xtravagance is the dot of the i confirmly that we are in the presence of topcat. Tophat was the sapphic pen by excellence worn by Dietrich, Colette, Romaine Brooks. Stovepipe Lincoln hid his papers in it. Aristocratic french women wore war ships in theirs to show their allegiance. Milliners such as Stephen Jones' Schiapirelli inspired swooping wings, fish skeleton, or this season's giant blue straw bicorne, Philip Treacy's live orchids, or the lime green acorn that grew out of a TV star, Shellie McDowell's large kettle brim hats,

Grace Jones's asymmetrical largesse. Kepen ones hat on: to refuse what's coming down, b on the up & up, a front to speak, sayeth yes to something else, wear it loud wear it high!

Halo

But 'tis the halo is the first headdress, the first cloak, much favoured by pilgrim companions. Like going to kirke and to chapelle 'tis obvious the centrally most memorable motif of attire is not the dress but the topping. Sacred riches coverchief antenna all in one. Frequently crushed from pigments xtracted and ground from precius minerals and lumps of shit from divine mountaingoates, gold leef, blue lapis, rede iron, or grene verdigris, rays of varying lengths shoot out from arounding the head in hundereth arrows. Or they burn contained within a dense Minerall circle. And this is how a highly saintly chakra may rise, like a funnel chignon or high bun, an irridiscent bouquet allrounding the skull, sign of great wisdam.

Aura

Once in awhile the current from a being is such that it jolte expande consciousness, even bypasse headbulbs. Just undertaking an anodyne action in the visible world such as greeting somebody, stretching ma hand to touch or hug them be travelling through many imperceptible theric layers melding both mine and hires body through a structure of threads and electricitee. By time we make contact, long beforen any resonant wilcuman, wellwishing, welcome be ye, all hail oure magnetic greeting has long taken place, yet oures perception of the full event remains dormant. These days the electromagnetic pollution from industrial and communication networks has invaded so much of our prospective space that the body's electric charge is distorted, threatening epileptic fits, shifting its long-term cellular balance, and many encounters are missed or misinterpreted. Whamo, current headwear being for protection against direct contact, informal knitcap bobblebeanies, worn with or without pompom and earflaps, worn outdoors and indoors, inunder large presence-cancelling soundflaps, we inbumpe one another widouten even noticing.

Dream vision

A vision of large halos arounding large seated figures at the centre of waves of cosmic oshun. Universe ycome manifest through the psychedelic circles of the figures electric presence.

Freud

"The aura given out by a person or object is as much a part of them as their flesh" writ Freud, Lucian the great exilic paintour. "The effect they make in space is as bound up with them as might be their colour or smell. The effect in space of two different individuals can be as different as the effect of a candle and an electric light bulb".

Aye but notes Ali, such awful depressing portraits, the splayed or curled up naked bodies, the whelping dogs, the tired anointed queens, all emerge from same low greay skies, like the limey green claustrophobia of an English climate in eternal post-war brexed-out climate. All within the cruel restrictions of socialisation and bad skin. One has survived but for what.

No chromatic range

No splash

No outburst

No breakthrough

No flight

No leakage

No energy

No random red

No glimmer

No hat!

No life but here, and this is no life.

To this levelling of the face would gladly envisage other disturbing vistas. For ensemple me piache the violent faceless queer theatricality of Leigh Bowery, the desperate runny portraits of Marlene Dumas, the intense mourning of Martha Garham's faceless dance sculptures, the bizarre organic reenactments of Cindy Sherman. Or be enjoyed by the enlivening turquoise of Roni Horn's Icelandic face, the full-frontal collaged encouragement of Thomas Mickalenes black pride sisterhood.

Dream click

The aura, quod Susan Hiller artist, is a working tool for digital identities, what the eye can't see, photographye's clairvoyant capacity captures spectral anatomies. Indeed, warms Marina thoughtfully, thinker of fantastic metamorphoses, such hauntings and technological sightings illuminate a new model of subjectivity. "One, she says, where the person is not a singleton, but a node in a web of connections".

And

In the end, whether it is of the fantasised and invisible protective space, or of the technological record, or of the colores hemselves, what mattere when ywering ones chief is the sense of inhabiting the connection betweened seen and unseen, happened and happening, and of being in the middle of ones lyfes xpansive event.

Pilgrimming

It is during the wilde months of Summer, just about around
Aprils poetic promess, whan it is hotter than July, and the
aires jasmine enflamed, after the harsh monthe of Januarie
at the hert of Winteres grief ystricken lands, long after the
shifting crashing plates of Autumn's rains and its wacking
series of lunar tempests, that May's luscious soote blooming
calls & folks long to go on pilgrimming.

Large bandes of peoples take to the streets in a sea of flags &
banners, placards & slogans, blow trombones, shout mega-
fones, take boombooms to the parks, pilgrims be chained to
gates or downsail the commons carrying an outrage of de-
manding, & peaceful wheelchaired tipped over by police insit
befront parliament until all chairs be redressed. Bridges be

occupied with rebellion, squares and streets be occupied with rebellion, stations and airports with rebellion, time and rush hour be occupied with rebellion. Battling has a rage that grows in the collective heart, passions rekindle what were left unkind yesteryar. Walking with limbes and mindes, from cities to sites, occupyeth all what can be, tent up squares, burn to build bridges, re-own the city, wear armour if moost be, make them well-worne.

Let's celebrate congregate upbring the fever and collected energy, all the passionate, angered, urgent, demands of our crowded multifarious lives as we later take on and manifest the gr8 rethink:

how to organise

how to salvage

how to soulsearch

how to take back the confiscations

of the streets of the lands of the minds of our physical health and inner outer mobilities

how to kepe libraries squares bookes open and publik

how to make education matteren

how to change literacy to meet our changing needs and numbres how to retrain against fear isolation indolence

how to fight mysterious illnesses and lack of available care and healing

how to plan neighbourly life

how 2 grow more edibles out of tarmac allotments

how to wear locally ete locally growe mo locally

how to fucken progress is dangerously outlived outdone

how to live sloer lives, togethered cooperatively, open a tactitall hand, geteth going

prepeth whats coming, get skriking

how to accept to be formed changed strategically purposefully

how to transuse ones privileges diligently favoure broadening vantages

how to rejog frontiers form transnational gossips

respecte across borders and across the hertes

how to share translocally, njoy unfamiliar offerings

how to bypass official controllers when only prevent necessary involvement

and geteth planning, activating, convincing, engineering, and sustaining for one longfix with a thousand soluctions

how to reclaim political activision for gooding, for long-haul futuring, in smaller yet interactive ranges of connectings how to finally give good bootance all over the places getriddance of your own brand of nasties, romping depraved governing galleries of rats what pass for demockratly lected magpies, bunches of lech & griffs work only for the sake of their behind the scenes, bandit rascals corrupters beyond all hope of usefulness, get em good kickance offbooted intergalatically!

Gaptothed

Too right! exclaims Alisoun. We've kept seprate fronts for too long, seprate ponds seprate beds seprate ways 'n battles of kinds, together nat by kin nat by kind, all kings a drag anyhow, ignorance nis bliss. Operatively takes time takes aspiration, sending love out nis simpel matter, naming kept me stumm until I stepped off, until I let the heart speak for me with me, feeling the current rise as I do and the light of intention come warm and crisp. One by one I peel the layers & give thanks. Ne fetish love! Ne totemic love! I speak from the yoni in my Johnny. See, I'm gap-tothed I was, and that bicam me weel. The winds whistle thro ma lips when I speech and fortellen things even I didnt know.

Mind

A gap is not just th air btween teeth. Its that special nothing. The space that shows whats around whats not there. All there but where. Space nothinged. Unspace makes the spaceplace. SunRa knew the place.

Root support makes kende a type of seeing, the pain of a vast unhoming shapes all future rehoming. No place for home makes kende a type of unliving, make room.

The fallow time of a plot of dyrket jord. After and before ynourished by the lag.

Afterthought sees the future, but needs rescuing now nou nu!

A form of gender-gap xamines the interstices release the underbelly the cover-ups as much as the opening pleasure, the wider reach. What hasnt been tormented with sense.

It's the glass full of empty, its the inner spacechair, chair-space.

It's the— and the) (and the : and .

Molecular legs. Its the street btween standing bldings, between letters. A caroline script is in the gaps as much as in the caps and the rhythmical punctuation.

Room-sound inlets another worlde at the break.

Voices in sub-language, and languages beyond language, and language after languages.

I see gaps everywhere! Xlaims Alisoun enchanted. They the hiatus, the nterruption, the pothole, the sudn fla in the system what scuprs it all, the betweened what precedes what follows. Tis a lookie around what takes no for an ansir! identifies othre measurings for love and justice.

Sometimes an individual's momentary loss of patience expresses what millions yfeeling. A home-owner refuses to be dislodged by new developments, they build all around it. Try to upchoke it but for the tiny stubborn solitary plot.

Viv

Queen Vivienne, gap-tothed punk hirselfe, onwalks wearing lycra tights with a green sewn-on fig-leaf. A nothing of beaut. An unexpected whoa presses joy gainst the cheste. A gong midaire unrings the moment. And all whats agitates the inner being with smale constant offers of unravelling.

Mary Douglas

There's a darker gap story I wish to relay. The word gaet cognates with Old Frisian gat, jet, and means hole, opening or

Old Saxon of a needle, and in Low German means opening, passage. The Sanskrit hadati brings up defecate, and de Greek chézein defecate, from Indo-European ^ghed- ^ghod, hole, defecate. The early gap is borrowed from old Icelandic gap meaning chasm. The verb gapa å gape to openen the mutt in wonder surprise or disbelief. Of course, symbolically also means producer of foul language. A bod has orifices. And paraquoding Mary Douglas in her Purity and Danger it matters lite which orifice is used for which function. Each ritualistically protected only to be breached mo regularlie.

Harpooned

This talk of gaps has me got stirred, recuntes Alisoun. What memory is made of this, whan that it remembreth me! Many yards past, frog-torn had I been, appled to the core. Sense-lessle harpooned 4 hrs in a miserable barrack way outa quarters. Robbed mobbed disrobbed by a loud yob. Scremed and shouted, yfighted back like a fierce Turelure a rightall Marguerite. Wont be turned into no tree! Yob larffs angrily wah ha ha, chekout the slut, slams in evry hole evry stretcht pore. Turns out ma bods one giant chese, cunt believe his luck theres hols evrywhere on tis bitch fillitup! wants to outchoken mine w his misrabl leef feels protected by the lawe. Hit ma skull gainst the bord nere passed out. Outte me left ear starts a smal blood stream. Utta me right runne foamy thick creamy yelloish fluid of dead phagocytes, chiefle polymorpho-nuclear leukocytes and othere swich cellular debrikbraks, by and large pus infected fever, before passing out full length.

Unsounded

And ner again cleared ma ears.

Oaute you say?

Well, since then me left un is a lite corked as tho thumbed in, cottoned off. I hear niet nada or very lite of soft rustling cloth, of whisperings, of feet riddims on wooden flores, of the clare brihte tonations of distant voices, of the last fading chimes at the mirabelle, or the sighs of ma most welcome sixte loving paramour.

Pain

For a long time din know totally unsiker how to feel, what to feel, how 2 speak how 2 make sense of my oute nor inne forms, labouring w cramps nausea seems I kende bare bones about or getting agripped in the reaches, am flopping around, me spine fele as dead morte as a greyed coral reef. What patchwork of shadows have shaped ma limbes ma organs ma mynd concaving ma belly a muted drum. Was my body ever mine oh mine?

A sort of pain, not pain yet peine, and fear, binded my shapes within it, sealed me off, outlocked me by inlocking, brought in mo pain like a penalty for pain, everythink was pain, had pain, not pain yet pain, made of peyne, made salve in pain, armour of pain, traumatised to the cor, solitary confined, cramping up without warning, while opening a cupboard, standing at the bus stop, chatting to the postman, patterning new smocks, waking up crying out, in pain. Then dout grabs hold increeses fear eats out all selfes entre t liver t kidneys buils up bile camps up balloons fear flatulence trauma gas. Brr me gives kreepy to think on this!

Ah

Ah m' bite ah th' dust
Ah m' give ah th' creeps
Ah th' insult ah th' injury
Ah th' end ah th' road

Hildegard

Wise Hildegard finally on the scene takes a cue from Melody and other sciences & writs up a cure for such dark uncertain maladyes: "The soul then lies oppressed in body & waits, uncertain whether to leave the body or to remain. As soon as it senses the tempests of the livores, lessened a little by the grace of god, it gathers its powers and expels those humors from the body as sweat. In this way the person regains their health."

Gabfull

There are many ways of enforcing silence on a situation, kepen a lye on it, originally to lie w one's cap on, to cover, cover-up. Incl. Letting sleeping whelpes lie by shooting them in the head. Shutting the lawe down. Building up shame. Making it personal. Doing ones worstest ad kavanausea. Criminalising all formes of solidaritee. Dissuading assemblee. Reducing the legal numbres at assemblee. Calling a peaceful demonstation a riot. Under-reporting on the ground actions. Preventing citizens action. Preventing public speechers. Ridiculing unusual initiatives. Ridiculing gabfull women.

Many

In some communities where direct intervention is imposs-
ible women responden to severe domestic violence by assem-
ble outside the house and bang out alarms on pots and pans.
This informe the assailor what the spirit he try broken be-
longe to many, not one.

Collective poesy

Ah let's bang some pan! offget the desolation ybefallen this
tale. For a few pages forward, let's go to the 21 January 2017,
a day that instigated the long cold silencing about to be end-
lessly resisted:

21 January 2017

On the morning of the 21 january 2017
I get up get dressed shake off the shadows and get out
shake off the shadows
shake off the shadows
shake off the shadows
and get out

Breathe out out out
trapped fear and heartache

breathe out out out
grief naked memory wounding
breathe out incapacitating doubtful mind
Oh mine oh mine oh mine
into the crowded structure of the day

Arrive at this place of movement
this magnificent crowdmass clusters and masses
unfolding lines angry necessary lines in harsh times
parched from a need for joy
and the energies of the heart

Come out come
in, there is a journey
to the deep crowd, there is a journey
winding stretching long bell resonance
cellular breath living fighting frequency journey
from Washington to London Detroit Paris Leeds Athens
Oslo Berlin Dublin Helsinki Amsterdam Rangoon Madrid
Beirut New Delhi Rio de Janeiro Tokyo Macau Montreal Jo-
hannesburg Honolulu Bucarest Tuuk and
on and on and on and on no peripheral location today in this
rounded world this rounding world holding world multidi-

mensional fighting breathing world
Say yes girl!
Say yes sisbro!

Yes, says the sound of the crowd
says the sound of the voice who is not
my inner judge not my hungry
critic always in my ear crippling incapacitating stops
me at the door encourages procrastination numbness sorrow
disconnect
my fearful alienation indolence apathy solitary heartwrench

Yes, says the crowd joined-up protective marching
world embraced
fired up multidimensional interfloating underskin
while education rolls back, sexual rights roll back, asylum sup-
port rolls back, health care and benefits roll back, bilingual
laws roll back, public speech rolls back.

Yes, says the crowd
rich undertonal transiently femaled
transdimensional fighter inside outsider outside insider

specific to each of us
at work in all of us
makes itself heard makes itself felt
appears when absolutely needed
when I'm on my knees
when we're on our knees
on our knees on our knees on our knees on our knees

Yes, says the crowd
says the wave of the crowd
    says the sound of the voice of the crowd
free rider of the darkest times
bumper alonger for a bettering time
trickster believer
translocal unaffected by border controls
noisy singer of the false notes
yogini flash speed
traveller of the slowest resilienste pace
stirdiest station pelvic hold
loving satiating lover
pilot of the longest detours
dropper of things

Yes,

    says the voice

says the sound of the voice

says the feeling of the sound of the voice

not a voice but a space but a sound

Start walking

          yes

   keep

walking yes keep marching   breathing yes

says the feeling of the sound of the voices of the crowd

   Yes,

says the feeling of the sound of the voices of the crowd

like planting trees after trees

entire forests in the skinned ransacked hillsides of our minds.

Everything in the world began with a yes.

Long lines and being

long lines of beings lines and clusters of walking marching

beings walking in long lines

clusters of beings waiting walking marching beings

clamouring beings

growing into clusters collecting lines of thinking picking up
strength of being
in lines of sharing and believing
sharing and walking in long lines and clusters of beings

Marching into lines of history ruptures and violence along
lines of conventions and dominance
Long lines of beings and histories of species of beings con-
fined confiscated absented
Long lines as slow as walking and transforming
Walking and marching and waiting and waking
as slow as seeded growth clustered beings that walk aloud
march aloud breathe aloud

Walk aloud think aloud dream aloud
Believe in the lines that form and grow into clusters of beings
Clusters and lines of being
thinking aloud breathing aloud
Picking up what stumbles down the line
Picking you up where you fall down
Picking you up when you fall
picking me up when i fall when i doubt when i fear when i

stop when i cant move anymore
picking you up into lines and chains of arms
long lines and fields of beings
surf with other beings
for being with beings
makes lines with being.

We have hardly begun to relate and relay
in long lines of memory and clusters of beings
for the end of the line
is the end of differences
is the end of love
and the end of the line
is the end of elephants and trombones and forests.

Walk aloud think aloud dream aloud
believe in the lines that form and grow into clusters of beings
the walk that crosses the mind is a long line of light
of thinking aloud breathing aloud
picking up what stumbles down the line
picking you up where you fall down
picking you up when you fall

Everything in the world began with a Yes

Τα πάντα στον κόσμο ξεκίνησαν με ένα 'ναι'

بدأ كل شيء في العالم بكلمة نعم

Alles in der Welt begann mit einem Ja.

Tot en el món va començar amb un sí

Tudo no mundo começou com um sim

Declaration

To summarise and close in orderly fashion I have prepped a numbre pointes, says Alisoun nearing the ende her pretext. In short lines, hastens she, yit firm claration. But first left me reminde youse am a local lasse. Yes not rose nor trained articulat, yet a wyse woman with appetites. I have lived I live on. Yes I can structure not a full convolution yet fully intente revolutionise oure ways with the chances I take. So left me responde those who ventriloquise, gravely salivate over deals closed in their favour, ne leave a single pleat out theirs foldes, ne bloode noght disturb the way thinges be, wanten collective action come ready-done, art to be soold nat soulfood, action to shlock nat transform, keeping the market canned reminding ooh it's a good deal for som of the very fewy! Let me sayeth this justly:

Let me tell you how it is
art n poesy do change the worlds!
heal our hearts, complete our minds!
charge our lives, ground our fights!
in a minor scale for major impack
dreaming practicalised wit crafts n craft
word beyond word, fair bravery rapsodises
in the nude out on the streets cross all devices

Like hey say: Pump up the V
Dont believe the tag!
Mind's opulent compost poesy
Big up! Hystoricise!

Left me put it this way, I say it once mo:
Let gendre's bondage finally be done done!
power coupling be outdanced rebalanced
marriages annuled til betre used & understonded
make a liance of equaled, not property dealings
make family out of other queried modelings
and larger frameworks like rethinking the citee
for public spacings & speechings & sanctuary

Love is a friction of energy fields
of sexual textile gainst sexual
textile of mental tissue gainst mental
tissue beings interweave as they meet
Transformation of the genda
is a transformation of the worlde
biosex makes all kinds of flowerings
but the rest is cohabitation and cooperatings

For trewe human fertility
is in the fruitfulness of dialoges
in the nectar of joined forces
in the permeability of the intimately
the networked spirit of soul beings
against the isolation of the fear machine
the vertigo of wars, the overprod of ego needs
the indifferent prejudicial swindle of the racketeers

Rejecte the narrowness with which we are intended!
its accepted forms of shame and expectations
Let free our beings from hardened limitations
engage dreams, bolster tender tentacular realities

Courage grows when grown from love's justice
upcall and personate its wisdom vastness!
Pleasures hard to achieve beyond kama kama teknik
'tis a lifeswork to share & comprehend as a click

So do axe again, how things unX
how fear and sadness can be unCnoted
Axe what creates conneks what brought 2gathered
interwoven cellularly inseparate like tongues in a cos
O let me put it this way: What is somebody morphed
to the sign of a larger future, collectivised without
sacrifice, feminised without fear, all shades and
gradations freely be lit and animated

Like I said: Pump up the V
Dont believe the tag!
Mind's opulent compost poesy
Big up! Hystoricise

Yet how should we even be living now
if all the fisshes nor mammals nor insects
nor the last of the nomadic wilds begoned

Who will we be what will we singen without
the animals nor the human tongues
how shall we be sleeping be speaking
withouten bees parrotes nittegales nor owles
blackbriddes singing nomore in the deado niht?

In our dayes, still nothing but covetyse
poison manslughtre and mordre in any wyse
this last gasp is the pire what intensify
warring doctrines to the end of greed and tyranny
bait-politicks, bodies used for border fodder
wolde rather burn the earth to a crisp than deal
with the screaming volcanic birthpanges
of an inescapable gaian overload

Telle yous, tis hih time emurgency!
Salvage all what can be!
for a Demeter changeover rescue operation
I telle you the time is come nearly gone
for rightfull guardianship Real tuff
sharing out of our spherical garden

fill a mynd full of mischief, hardened wisdom
plough the fields for radical reunion of earthlings

O SIS! O SISIS!
YO SISISBRO! YO BROSIS!
YEY SISBROSIS! YEY BROSISBRO!
YALL BROSISBROBRO! YELL BROBROSISBROSIS!
YELL SISIS! YELL SISBRO!
Too many deals not nuf daring!
Too much lingo not enough tongue!
Too much fear not enough fyr!

Yes it is a difficult yet not impossible rethink
oure ways of living loving breathing giving
sitting ploughing watering earning feeding
bumping dreaming kneeling sharing flighting
Transform with Loki! breathe with Shakti!
make a concerted desperate purpous of simpler
connected living and get into bed with th'Earth
like a lovely and brave Mendieta

For in this, ma friendly companye

we are alle her kindren

alle in a melee

bearded unbearded alyking

and alle we must sharen

the callout and the song

Each of us updreamed as we be

from her round and sacred ground.

End of the Begin

At the ende of this meandering flow of amazonian magnifi-
cence, som electrified som transported give Alisoun a stand-
ing O! Whistling clapping some hold their hands high up
above their heads lighting a wave enthusiastikly. While predi-
catably som are shouting, "Hey missy, turn doun a notch",
spred insults, "kus like you have been chewing this for cen-
tries" and som more "your kind is crudes, lips smacked bab-
bling away rubbing wordes tween yous loosening the divine
with Salima's saliva and god knows anya else's breath." But
otheres of all kinds and kins, growing in numbres and con-
fidence at the end of one world, & its transitional concluding
momentum know the value of her storm, excited exhausted
pummeled in a goodway like fully thai massaged both flesh
heart and soul, look down on smartfony & sighen: "PHEW!
but it's a long piece o' string!"

Welle, quod Alisoon, obligingly, yes it is a very long piece of string, a very very long piece of string. How many warps for how many wefts will it take to weave this into our senses. How many hands to move mountains! How many furlongs in 18 thousand words! How many stars borne from a a revolutionary galactical orgasm! a dames rallying cry!

Or put more simply: How much blood guts and perspiration to finally transpire! How many individuals to collectivise! To relay a profounding relay! How many notes to make opera! How much opera to make operative!

And for those of yous who bethink me all forsongen?

Abyde! quod Alisoun, all good king's in drag! The era of ma tellings nat bygone, just bigonne.

Alisoun Sings (1389 2019)

Notes

Yoni: Songs

Madonna, Like A Virgin

Missy Elliott, Get Ur Freak On

Marvin Gaye, Sexual Healing

PJ Harvey, Dress

Elton John, Saturday Night's Alright

Parliament, I've Been Watching You (The Way You Move Your Sexy
   Bodey)

Chakha Khan & Rufus, Ain't Nobody

Nina Simone, Do I Move You

Outkast/Love Below, Spread

Me'Shell Ndegeocello, Andromeda

Yo Majesty, Don't Let Go

Thelma Houston, Don't Leave Me This Way

Grace Jones, Pull Up to the Bumper

Kelis, Good Stuff

Donna Summer, I Feel Love

Madonna, Justify My Love

Missy Elliott, Sock iT 2 Me

Anita Ward, Ring My Bell

Kylie Minogue, Just Can't Get You Out of My Head

Siouxie and the Banshees, Obsession

Peggy Lee/The Cramps, Fever

Baby D, I Wanna Be Your Fantasy

KD Lang, Constant Craving

Sonic Youth, Kissability

ABBA, Honey Honey

Pointer Sisters, I'm So Excited

Bessie Smith/Nina Simone, Sugar in My Bowl

Kelis, Milkshake

Temptations, Do Your Thing

Magnetic Fields, Underwear

Diana Ross, Upside Down

Catpower, I've Been Thinking

Serge Gainsbourg, Marilou

Justin Timberlake, Futuresex

PJ Harvey, Oh My Lover

Prince, I Would Die 4 U

Patti Smith, Frederick

Robert Wyatt, Sea Song

Cole Porter, Night and Day

Björk, Unison

Le Tigre, Eau d'Bedroom Dancing

Patti Smith, Because the Night

Sonic Youth, Star Power

Kate Bush, Hounds of Love

Soft Cell, Soul Inside

Jah Wobble & Sinaed O'Connor, Visions of You

Skin, One Thousand Years

Emmylou Harris, May This Be Love

Nick Cave, Into My Arms

Ewan McColl/Roberta Flack, The First Time Ever I Saw Your Face

Al Green/ Queen Latifah, Simply Beautiful

SNAP, Rhythm Is a Dancer

Björk, All Is Full of Love

Grace Jones, Slave to the Rhythm

Serge Gainsbourg / Catpower, Je T'aime (Moi Non Plus)

The Beatles, Strawberry Fields

Janelle Monae, Electric Lady

Bookes: Texts & Names

Christine de Pizan, *La Querelle du Roman de la Rose,* 1402

Diane Abbott, British MP, outspoken about severe and constant racist abuse to herself and her family

Jo Cox, British MP, outspoken about tolerance and immigration, murdered by Far Right white extremist, June 2016

Mary Beard, *Women and Power: A Manifesto*, 2017

Patti Smith, "Piss Factory", 1974

Kathy Acker, *Bodies of Work*, 1996

Octavia Butler, *Parable of the Sower,* 1993 *Parable of the Talents,* 1998

Judith Butler, *Giving an Account of Oneself,* 2005

Valerie Solanas, *SCUM Manifesto,* 1967

Adundhati Roy, *End of the Imagination,* 2016

Hannah Arendt, *Men in Dark Times*, 1968

Erin Moure, *O Cidadan,* 2002 *O Cadoiro,* 2007

Mina Loy, "A Manifesto", 1914

Donna Haraway, *Staying with the Trouble: Making Kin in the Chthulucene,* 2017

Kate Tempest, *Let Them Eat Chaos*, 2016

Inger Christensen, *It*, 1969 transl. from Danish by Suzanne Bier (1971)

Monique Wittig, *Les Guérilllères*, 1969 transl. from French by David Le Vay (1971)

Virginie Despentes, *King Kong Theory,* 2006

Emma Goldman, *Living my Life*, 1931

Structure from Monique Wittig, *Les Guérilllères*

Angela Davis, *Freedom is a Constant Struggle: Ferguson, Palestine, and the Foundations of a Movement,* 2016

Etel Adnan, *Sea and Fog,* 2012

Rebecca Solnit, *Hope in the Dark: Untold Histories Wild Possibilities*, 2004

Isabelle Stengers, *In Catastrophic Times: Resisting the Coming Barbarism*, tr. into English Andrew Goffey (2015)

Nicole Brossard, *La Lettre Aérienne*, 1985 transl. from French (1987)

Audre Lorde, *Sister Outsider: Essays and Speeches,* 1984

Anne Waldman, *Jaguar Harmonics,* 2014

Cecilia Vicuña, "Language is Migrant", 2017

Maya Angelou, *I Know Why the Caged Bird Sings,* 1969

Virgina Woolf, *A Room of One's Own,* 1929

June Jordan, *On Call: Political Essays,* 1985

Hélène Cixous, *La Jeune Née,* 1974 *Three Steps on the Ladder of Writing*, 1994

Rodney McMillian, "Untitled" artwork 2008, Whitney Biennial

Nancy Spero, "Codex Artaud" artwork 1973, "Torture of Women", artwork 1976

Judith M. Bennett, *History Matters*, 2007

Hildegard von Bingen, *Causae et Curae*, 1100

Mary Douglas *Purity and Danger: An Analysis of Concepts of Pollution and Taboo,* 1966

Other heroes named here are Glenn Ligon, Suzanne Lacy, Adrian Piper, Susan Hiller, Christian Boltanski, Chelsea Manning, Ed Snowden, Leshia Evans, Carol Cadwalladr, Pier Paolo Pasolini . . .

Clarice Lispector's Yes—opening line of *A Hora de Estrela*: "Tudo no mundo começou com um sim" translated by Nina Rapi (Greek), Samira Negrouche (Arabic), Uljana Wolf (German), Erin Moure (Catalan).

Stitch: Fabrics & Articles

Margaret Scott, *Fashion in the Middle Ages*, 2011

Sarah Thursfield, *Medieval tailors assistant: Making common garments 1200–1500*, 2001

Eleanora Cards-Wilson, "Haberget: A Medieval Textile Conundrum", 1968: "It clearly denoted a cloth that could be made in several different qualities—for Becket's cloak as made of 'fine' haubergie; that was worn by people of very different rank socially".

Abigail Westover, *Medieval 1100–1450 / History of Costume*, posts about medieval fashion

Thoreau, *Walden*, 1854

Emma Goldman, seamstress, anarchist, political activist, strike leader, public speaker, feminist

Clara Lemlich, leader Shirtwaist Workers Strike, 1909

Bill Haywood and Elizabeth Gurley Flynn, leaders Lawrence Textile Strike, also known as Bread and Roses Strike, 1912

As we come marching, marching, we battle too for men,
For they are women's children, and we mother them again.

Our lives shall not be sweated from birth until life closes;

Hearts starve as well as bodies; give us bread, but give us roses!

(James Oppenheim, 1911)

Sandy Black, *The Sustainable Fashion Handbook*, 2013

Kate Fletcher, et al *Fashion and Sustainability: Design for Change*, 2012

Pietra Rivoli, *The Travels of a T-Shirt in the Global Economy: An Economist Examines the Markets, Power, and Politics of World Trade. New Preface and Epilogue with Updates on Economic Issues and Main Characters*, 2014

Lucy Siegle, *To Die For: Is Fashion Wearing Out The World?*, 2011

Claire Wilcox, *Vivienne Westwood*, 2005

Vivienne Westwood, *Get a Life: The diaries of Vivienne Westwood*, 2010

Sass Brown, *ReFashioned: Cutting-Edge Clothing from Upcycled Materials*, 2013

Carlo Petrini & John Irving, *Food & Freedom: How the Slow Food Movement Is Changing the World through Gastronomy*, 2015

Lucy + Jorge Orta, "Refuge Wear," artwork 1996–2003

Lucy + Jorge Orta, "Body Architecture", artwork 1994

Krzysztof Wodiczko, "Porte-Parole Mouthpieces (Xenological Instrument)", artwork 1995

Mona Hatoum, "Keffieh", artwork 1993–99

Mona Hatoum w/ Inaash, "Twelve Windows", 12 Palestinian Embroideries, artwork 2012–13

Alex Martin, "The Little Brown Dress" artwork, 2006

Marie Ange Guilleminot, "Le Paravent", artwork 2018

Thanks

A book is made of many books. And many hands and minds and skills assist its unique making. A very early version of this text came out as a small chaplet in 2008 in an edition of 75 copies. Thank you to its publishers Belladonna for initiating this project's first step and to Dia Art Foundation, NY, where it was performed that same night as a short one-off concert with guitarist Mario Diaz de Léon. Nearly ten years passed before I picked up what had been started and decided to transform this initial address into a fully fledged poetic voice. Thank you to all those who helped me through what turned out to be an extremely demanding, all-consuming writing process. Much gratitude to my attentive, precise, enthustiastic yet hard-nosed critical readers, friends of Alisoun, you each helped me find her, feed her and then let her loose: Clare Lees, David Wallace, Susan Rudy, Rachel Lichtenstein, Rachel Levitsky and as always, Erin Moure. To my editor at Nightboat, Lindsey Boldt, and to Jeff Clark for the book's design, my thanks to you both for genuine patience and care. To my publisher Stephen

Motika for providing me with all the encouragement and the amazing slack I needed to bring this to completion, much later than planned yet nonetheless just on time thanks to you. And finally, a few words to you, dear reader, dear listener, now that you are at the end of these pages: Should you have found yourself caught in the pleasures of this encounter, sometimes blissed out, at others provoked, yet made ready to pick up the baton and respond in your ways to her call, I will consider that Alisoun's use of me is done.

Caroline Bergvall

is a writer of French-Norwegian origins based in London. She works across art-forms, media and languages. Her outputs alternate between books, collaborative performances and language installations. Award winning poet and performer, her publications include *Drift* (recipient of the Cholmondeley Award for Poetry 2017), *Meddle English: New and Selected Texts* (recently translated into the French: *L'Anglais Mêlé*), *Fig* (2005) and the DVD *Ghost Pieces: five language-based installations* (2010). She is the first recipient of the art literary prize Prix Littéraire Bernard Heidsieck-Centre Pompidou, Paris (2017). Recent works and commissions include: Documenta14 (Kassel), John Hansard Gallery (Southampton), Dublin International Literature Festival, The Whitstable Biennale (UK), Palais de Tokyo (Paris), ICA (Portland), The Jewish Museum (Munich), Festival de la Batie (Geneva), Tate Modern (London). Her widely reviewed work *Ragadawn* (2016-2020) is an outdoor sunrise performance for spoken voice, soprano and a dawn chorus of voices in multiple minoritarian languages (with vocal work by British composer Gavin Bryars). She was the director of the interdisciplinary program in Performance Writing at Dartington College of Arts (1995–2000), co-Chair of the MFA in Writing at Bard College (2005–2007), a Whitechapel Gallery Writer-in-Residence (2014), a Collaborative Fellow at The University of Chicago (w/ Jen Scappettone & Judd Morrissey, 2016), a recent guest faculty at Naropa University, and the Judith E. Wilson Fellow in Poetry and Drama at the University of Cambridge (2012–2013). She is currently a Visiting Professor in Medieval Studies at King's College London.

Nightboat Books

Nightboat Books, a nonprofit organization, seeks to develop audiences for writers whose work resists convention and transcends boundaries. We publish books rich with poignancy, intelligence, and risk. Please visit nightboat.org to learn about our titles and how you can support our future publications.

The following individuals have supported the publication of this book. We thank them for their generosity and commitment to the mission of Nightboat Books:

Kazim Ali

Anonymous

Jean C. Ballantyne

Photios Giovanis

Amanda Greenberger

Elizabeth Motika

Benjamin Taylor

Peter Waldor

Jerrie Whitfield & Richard Motika